Life Among the
Qallunaat

Life Among the Qallunaat

Minnie Aodla Freeman

Hurtig Publishers
Edmonton

Copyright © 1978 by Minnie Aodla Freeman

No part of this book may be reproduced or transmitted in any form by any means, electronic or mechanical, including photocopying and recording, or by any information storage or retrieval system, without written permission from the publisher, except for brief passages quoted by a reviewer in a newspaper or magazine.

Hurtig Publishers
10560 – 105 Street
Edmonton, Alberta

Canadian Cataloguing in Publication Data

Freeman, Minnie Aodla.
    Life among the Qallunaat

    ISBN 0-88830-164-2

    1. Freeman, Minnie Aodla.   2. Eskimos –
Canada – Biography I. Title.
E99.E7F74   971' .004'97   C78-002128-2

Printed and bound in Canada

To
Milton
Graham
Elaine
and
Malcolm

Teach, learn, care and love while you can
for nothing ever stays the same.

Love,
Moms

Contents

Foreword

The 1950s saw an era of rapidly increasing public interest in Canada's vast northland. World War II had broken down the barriers of distance and communication. The North was no longer a remote area, accessible only to a limited number of southerners. The native people were no longer living in the isolation of their past way of life. The government of the day enunciated a policy of greater emphasis on northern development and particularly on the human needs — health, education and a sound economy — of northerners.

Staff in various disciplines were recruited: teachers, welfare and project officers, equipment mechanics and, in 1955-56, northern service officers, who eventually became area administrators coordinating the various department programs in the field. This was all part of the federal government's policy to help the Inuit cope with the transition and to ease the trauma of the celerity of the changing Arctic. Whether it was a good approach or not is a subject for debate; the Inuit way of life had been disrupted and a culture undermined. Yet there was a conscious effort to discharge this obligation to them and to raise their standard of living, which, in the wisdom of the day, was based on southern criteria.

Tuberculosis had found fertile ground among the Inuit people. In 1956 some 1600, or one in seven Inuit, were in various southern sanatoria, receiving treatment for tuberculosis. The movement of Inuit away from their homes and families appeared heartless to many. Treating the body was necessary, but removal from the Arctic created additional problems of the mind. Going to hospitals in the South was a strange and lonely experience, especially for Inuit who spoke little or none of any other language but their own. Why not hospitals nearer home? The answer was that even if enormous funds were spent on northern hospitals, treatment of tuberculosis could never be as effective as in southern medical centres where highly qualified specialists and sophisticated equipment and treatment techniques were readily available.

The forerunner of the present Department of Indian and Northern Affairs, with the overall responsibility for the welfare of the Inuit, was naturally concerned about the social and psychological effects on these patients in southern hospitals, as well as on their families in the North. As part of a massive program against tuberculosis, the staff of the Welfare Division of the department developed a "medical social services program." This would require not only professional social workers but also Inuit to work with their own people as translators and counsellors. There would be, as part of the program, the visiting of hospitals and the setting up of a system of communication between patients and their families by letters and tape recorded messages. Were there Inuit available who might work in this area which was coordinated from headquarters in Ottawa? Some experience in hospitals would be a valuable asset. A canvass was made and this is where Minnie Aodla entered the scene. Minnie and a few others were engaged, and they played a vital role in easing the pain of trying experiences for both patients and families.

Minnie was twenty when she joined the department in 1957. Born on the Cape Hope Islands of James Bay, she had learned English at the Anglican mission school on the mainland at Fort George. Later, as a patient at Moose Factory, her linguistic ability and her warm, pleasant personality lead the staff there to ask her to remain as a hospital employee. This she did for a short time. Then, with an increasing number of patients being moved south for treatment, National Health and Welfare officials invited her to transfer to Mountain Sanitorium in Hamilton. Here she became a nurse's aid and assisted in both translation and interpreting. It was from here that she went to Ottawa to join the Welfare Division and to work in the new medical social services program.

Although statistics do not always reflect every aspect of a situation, it is interesting to note that within six years a government report stated that the number of Inuit in southern institutions receiving medical treatment had dropped to 350. The incidence of tuberculosis had fallen dramatically and many patients were returning home. There were some sad letters to write, but how worthwhile and gratifying it must have been for Minnie and her colleagues to prepare correspondence in the Inuit language or tapes for radio messages notifying relatives of the patient's progress or better still, plans for him or her to return north to the home community, cured.

I well remember Minnie as a confident and attractive young lady. Her writings, however, reflect that Minnie herself faced considerable difficulties and misunderstandings in her introduction to Ottawa and other areas of southern Canada. In this enchanting book, which reveals much of her sincere and open manner, she now tells the story of her life some twenty years ago and of her childhood in the North.

Further to her credit and that of her people, she joins a growing number of Inuit who in recent years have expressed themselves in writing. It was only a short time ago that books about Inuit were written by non-Inuit. Minnie, by committing the experiences of her life to pen and paper, has made a fine contribution to Canadiana, helping, I hope, to bring about a better understanding of Canada's multi-cultural society.

Alex Stevenson
Former Administrator of the Arctic

Ottawa
April 1978

Qallunaaq (singular); *qallunaat* (plural): literally "people who pamper their eyebrows"; possibly an abbreviation of *qallunaaraaluit*: powerful, avaricious, of materialistic habit, people who tamper with nature.

I
Ottawamillunga:
In Ottawa

Whenever a white person meets me for the first time he or she will always ask, "How do you like the weather?" The weather is something I am very aware of, just as I am aware of many things which the *qallunaat,* the white people, take for granted. Surely people in the South must have more interesting questions than "How do you like the weather?"

There are countless things in the South which fascinate me. When I first arrived in Ottawa in 1957 and stepped down from the train at Union Station, my mind had many questions. Seeing the train tracks, I asked myself: am I supposed to walk on them or shall I walk on the cement? Which gateway shall I use? Is there a special door for arriving people?

My first ride in a car left me speechless. There were cars and more cars everywhere I looked; some were moving, some were parked. How does the man who is driving know when to stop and when to go? Does he count to a certain number? Or does the other car let him know? The blinking red light on the car ahead of us meant nothing to me. While my mind struggled with these mysteries, my driver asked about the weather during the trip.

I was taken to Laurentian Terrace, my Ottawa residence. Its high ceilings made me feel like a little ant. Why all the sofas and chairs, pictures on the walls and so many doors? The matron of the Terrace asked me to sit down. Which chair? I chose the nearest one. Little did I know I was to sit there for an hour, reading the rules I was to follow, rules and more rules that made me feel I could not move unless I was told. Rules are things we Inuit children were never brought up with; we ate when we were hungry, slept when we were tired, came and went with the weather. If it was a nice day, we hunted food and if it was a bad day, we stayed home — the women to sew, the men to work with their tools, the children to learn from their parents.

As I walked down the hall with the matron, she showed me the bathroom. Is this one mine? Later, I found out I was to share it with 300 girls. "This is the telephone you will be called on." Who is going to call me? How will anyone know I am here? Finally, after endless steps, she said, "This is your room. The rules are to change your bed once a week. Here is your key, lock your room when you leave. Here is the key for your locker, don't lose the combination." What a difference from living in a tent! We come and go with no locks and no combinations to remember.

I met the girl who was to share my room. She was very surprised by my hairdo; apparently it was out of date and too long. But she was more surprised that my clothes were as up to date as hers. When I began to unpack she left, but before long others came in, five or six different girls. To my embarrassment, she had invited them to see what kind of clothes I had, and they expected to be shown sealskin clothing, along with a folding igloo perhaps. When I got to the bottom, one of them asked, "Where are your clothes?" I wanted to laugh and say, as to any well-known friend, what do you mean? I have been putting them in this locker. One of them insisted, "Where are your own clothes?" and I replied, there, pointing to the locker. But she kept on insisting, "Where are your, you know, clothes where you come from? Skins." She practically spat out the word and her face had an ugly look. It was too much for me. Finally, one of the girls saw my discomfort and said, "How awful we are, watching her unpack." The others took the hint, said goodnight and left.

First Day At Work

I had come to Ottawa as a translator for the federal government, for what was then the Department of Northern Affairs and National Resources in May of 1957. My first months in the South were trying days, especially because of my shyness. Meeting five to ten people every day was agony for me. I could never look at them and I would barely say hello. To be honest, I don't really know why I was shy. It was not that I was ashamed of myself or that I was aware of my different colouring; having been brought up among Indian people, I was told to ignore differences of race and to treat all equally.

The first day of work I will never forget. The matron had told me that a woman would call for me. What would she look like? I stood for some time where I had been told to wait. Suddenly, a woman approached me. She said, "I can't remember your name, but are you the Eskimo?" I just nodded and followed her out.

I watched her walk ahead of me and thought to myself, she is so old and nothing seems to bother her. There is so much to see and yet she is not interested. Probably she has only one thing on her mind — her destination. When we arrived, I took my first ride in an elevator. The woman just punched a button and up we went. Will I have to do the same thing later? What will I say to make it go, or what will I think? Shall I just push a button like she did? I was not afraid of it, but very nervous to use it alone. I always made sure I went in with somebody else; no matter if it went up or down, somehow I always reached my floor.

My first day at work was very tiring. The man in charge of the division where I was to be a translator introduced me around, and I felt angry at him for doing so. Being very shy, introductions were the last thing I wanted, yet I was made to face person after person. I wanted to cry and just stay in one place. The desk I was given to sit at was my greatest comfort that day. I never left it, no matter how much I wanted to. Finally, I met the lady who showed me the rules of the office, and at the end of the day she walked back with me to Laurentian Terrace.

Lost

I had no problem going to work, but one frightful day I had to walk home alone. I had paid little attention to the names of the streets, but would go by the shapes of stores or commercial signs. Such was how I had learned to find my way in my culture; our style of travel demanded it. Passing the Chateau Laurier every day I saw a big sign, "Red Feather Week," over its door and knew that I was heading in the right direction. But one day the sign was gone and suddenly all the buildings looked the same to me. I walked and walked. I was getting very hungry. Then I remembered a friend in the North who had told me that I should never go to a stranger but always look for a policeman, a man in a navy blue uniform and hat with a peak. My friend was right; they were not hard to find. There was one standing on the corner of the street, just as my friend had described him. I went up to him rather shyly and asked if he could tell me where Sussex Street was. Up that way, he said, ten blocks! I wanted to ask him what had happened to the Red Feather Week sign, but I told myself that I would never go by it or any signs again, other than street names.

I never felt so relieved when I finally got home. I looked at the clock as I entered; I had been walking for two hours. Supper hour had passed. I entered my room, where my roommate was lying on her bed.

"Minnie, what happened to you? Did you have to work late?" I tried to explain. "Minnie, you could have been kidnapped or raped!" My head was shaking and nodding, trying to keep up with her questions. When she finally slowed down I had to admit I had been lost. She reminded me that supper hour was over; if I wanted anything to eat I would have to go out to a restaurant or bring the food back to our room. I was hungry, but did not feel like eating. I could not face the streets again. That night was not the last that I went to bed hungry, nor was it the last time I got lost.

I always took care to cross the street on a red light as I thought the cars would be alerted by the light and see me much clearer. But every time I crossed, cars would honk and I would wonder why. And no matter that there were ten or fifteen people standing on the corner with me, not one took time to tell me that I should not cross on the red light. It was not explained to me until weeks later when I became friends with another girl who lived at the Terrace. How I longed to step out of a tent and turn in any direction, without having to look for some kind of beast, ready to crush me if I didn't stay out of his way.

Stranger; how odd is the meaning of that word and yet that is what I was in my own country. It is a word I never heard used in my own language. Even white people have a beautiful Inuit name, qallunaat — "people who pamper their eyebrows." After two months I decided that the qallunaat were the saddest, most worried and most hurried, never-smiling people. It seemed that my parents wasted their time telling me, "If you have nothing to say, smile." I could neither speak nor smile in the South.

Unfamiliar Child-rearing

I began to meet a lot of people. My first visit to a qallunaat family and first long ride by car were exhausting. While in the car I did not know what to look at. There were other cars, buildings and stores. And there were people standing about, others walking as if they had big loads on their backs, though they carried only small bags in their hands. The man who was driving told me that he had just learned to drive. This surprised me; I thought he had known how to drive since childhood, just as I knew how to hitch a dog team at the age of five.

The home of the qallunaat family held more surprises. I noticed the children at once. They were not allowed to be normal, free to move, free to ask questions, or free to think aloud. In my culture children are encouraged to speak. As they grow older, questioning becomes a boring habit; they have gained wisdom and eventually become more intelligent. The more intelligent they become, the quieter they are. That is the reason Inuit children are allowed to be children. Qallunaat who have gone north and lived in the settlements, who do not understand Inuit home life or believe in our way of child-rearing, think that Inuit children are spoiled.

When I entered this *qallunaat* home, I could not help but notice the treatment of the children by the parents. One child asked, "Who is that girl?" She was answered with whispers and told to leave. Instead of being proud that the child was curious, instead of considering the way the child used her words, the parents silenced her immediately. To my people, such discipline can prevent a child from growing mentally, killing the child's sense of interest. "Is it very cold where she comes from? Did she live in an igloo before she came here?" Shhhh! the mother was cautioning. "Go outside! Don't do that! Move away!" How I wanted to pick up the child and say, "It is not very cold where I come from because we wear warm clothes." But words like "don't," "no," "move" were to me like talking to a dog who was eating from some other dog's dish or who did not obey commands given during sled travel. My culture tells me that the word no leads to disobedient children who become very hard to handle later on. My visit that day was an event, though I could not express my thoughts and feelings. Being very shy, all I said was yes, no and thank you.

Many Reasons for Loneliness

My weekends and evenings were often lonely. At times I would just lie on my bed, wishing I was with my family, and out of nowhere tears would come down my cheeks. I missed friends, open air, howling dogs, even the chores I had had to do — washing, cleaning, cutting wood, filling the water pails. I missed the sound of the sea just a few feet from our home, gathering twigs from the shore, welcoming a dog team just back from a hunting trip and most of all joking, laughing and smiling through these everyday events. I missed my food, especially frozen seal liver with seal fat. I missed going out on canoe trips to pick berries and the smell of tea brewed on an open fire.

I missed my brother, with whom I shared all these chores. His letters would make me cry. "I do all the work alone now. Today I put up snares; I am still allowed to use one dog but I miss your help pushing the sled." I could just picture him. He had to get up as soon as he opened his eyes because of our culture's tradition that we not lie around. That can lead to difficulty in bringing up children, and for a girl it means that she will have hard times while giving birth. We were never allowed to eat before we went outside. Grandmother would remind us, "Go out, look at the world, greet and admire your outdoor surroundings." Having to do this every day in our childhood became a joke to me and my brother. We would burst out laughing. What were we looking for? Grandmother always knew that we were laughing at something that we were not supposed to, and she would warn us that we would bear unhealthy children. Naturally we would be scared and try not to laugh at anything again.

I Knew Him and Yet Did Not

I joined the church's young people's association. My first meeting with the group was very happy. The minister who lead the group looked familiar and I guess he felt the same about me. Upon repeating my name and asking if I had ever been to Moose Factory, he realized who I was and I too began to remember. As we talked, I discovered that he had been my teacher at St. Thomas School in Moose Factory in 1941-2 and 1942-3. I had been too young to say that I knew him well. I knew him and yet did not, and he too knew me and yet not the young woman I had become.

I sat through the whole meeting and observed everything that was said and done. Various people were invited to speak about other countries. When my turn came I could not believe that I would stand up in front of all those people to speak. I put my hands in my shirt pockets, my legs swayed back and forth, and I stared at the floor. I spoke about Christmas, that we did not give gifts at Christmas, but on New Year's Day. They began to ask questions when I only wished it were over. Whenever anybody asked me about home, I just wanted to cry, missing it so much. They asked me to speak longer than I wanted to, and this was when my image of the *qallunaat* collapsed. I used to think they knew everything, were capable of anything, could change all things from bad to good. And most of all, I thought they knew all about the Inuit. All of the *qallunaat* who had come to my land had that attitude. But here all they knew was that it was cold in the North, that Inuit rub noses — and even then they thought that we caress with our noses like they caress with their lips. Sooner or later came the question I had learned to expect: "How do you like the weather?"

My Clothes Were Valuable

Washing my clothes taught me that nothing was free in the South. I remember going down to the basement with my *qallunaaq* friend. I expected to see a washing board; instead, I saw a square, white box. I watched my *qallunaaq* friend but asked no questions. She took it for granted that I knew how to operate the machine. Not a word was spoken as I copied her actions. I put in my clothes, added soap, inserted a quarter and away it went. I expected never to see my clothes again. While we waited my friend said that she wished they had a dryer. What is a dryer? All this time I thought they had a wash line outside. I even pictured myself standing out in a breeze and my washing shaking gently in the fresh air. Later, when we went to get our clothes, she showed me the wash line — in another room in the basement! The thought of smelling like musty, grey cement hung in my mind. I was told to be careful not to leave my clothes there too long or they would be stolen. Who would want to steal my clothes? At home I was taught never to steal, and surely *qallunaat* would not do that either. But in the evening, when I went for my clothes, two pairs of my panties, two pairs of nylons and a slip were missing. Nothing is impossible. Missionaries themselves stressed that stealing was a sin, and I was given the impression that *qallunaat* do not commit sins. To this day my friend does not know that I had never run an automatic washing machine before that day. And I often wonder why her underwear was not valued highly enough to be stolen.

So Close Together and Yet So Far Apart

My first ride on a bus during rush hour made me wonder how the bus could move with all its passengers. When I travelled with my family, the sled would not move if it was too full; the dogs could not budge it without help. But the bus, run by a motor, was something else. I was with a man and we were on our way to visit his family. I sat while he stood, but felt rather awkward as I was taught to let my elders sit, man or woman. Much later I learned that it was his custom to be a gentleman to a female, young or old.

No one spoke. Now and then I would hear a little bell and I learned that the bell meant that somebody was getting off. (I decided I would never ride the bus alone, because I would be too shy to ring the bell.) It occurred to me that people can be close together and yet far apart. No one seemed to know any other. I could not understand how people could ignore each other when they were sharing a bus, let alone one seat. While the bus lulled me into daydreams, making my mind drunk with the smell of gasoline, I thought of big gatherings at home. When a whale or seal was divided among the families, children laughed and threw stones into the water, dogs yapped and everybody enjoyed the food. I could hear the water at the shore and the merriment down the banks.

Exciting for a Qallunaat Girl

One day I stopped off at the mail office (another routine I had to get used to), and I picked up a strange looking envelope. Its contents told me to vote. What is vote? Why am I to vote? I did not understand it; I had never heard of it. My qallunaaq, who was younger than I, said to me that I was lucky, that she had to wait another four years before she could vote. She was very excited about it but I could not see any reason why. What is vote? What do I do? Who is the person I have to vote for? My qallunaaq told me where I had to go, that there were two men whose names would be written on a piece of paper, and that I should try to put an X on the right line or it would not count. What would not count? If I put it below or above the line? Who were these two men? What were they? I went to vote but still did not understand. Putting an X on a piece of paper was something I did not find exciting.

Keep Your Houses Clean

I began to take walks by myself, and my favourite spot was behind Parliament Hill, near the water. There all the memories of home would come to mind. Many times I would sit on a stone and tears would fall. I pictured a tent near the shore and heard waves smacking against canoes. I yearned to get pails and pails of water for drinking or for next day's wash. But the water I gazed at did not look normal at all. I would wonder why *qallunaat* stressed to Inuit people that they keep their houses clean, when the water right in their backyard looked so filthy. When I returned my *qallunaaq* would ask me where I had been and why. What did I see there? Somehow I could never explain. I had no words to tell her that somehow it made me feel at home to hear water smacking against the shore.

I Would Like to See to Whom I Am Talking

When I was first shown the telephone at Laurentian Terrace I had wondered who would call me. I had never really thought much about this machine and it took me ages to think of using it. At the office where I worked, I was often alone during lunch hours. Occasionally the phone, which sat next to my desk, would ring — always when I was alone it seemed. I ignored it. I would not know what to say if I picked it up. In fact I felt awkward about talking to someone I could not see.

It was one of those days when I was alone and the telephone started to ring. This time it would not stop. It got to the point that I could not ignore it. I thought of leaving the office, but on leaving I would have to pass it. I felt a bit ridiculous about my plan. Finally,

I decided to answer and told myself that whoever was wanted was not there; I would simply say so and hang up fast. I do not know how I sounded from the other end, but the voice said, "Speak up, Minnie, I cannot hear you." The voice I recognized! "I thought you would never answer," it said. "Minnie, it is only me. Wait, I will hang up and come over. I am just across the hall."

It was the lady who had been taking me various places for civil service tests. It was one of her tests. She explained to me how to answer, take messages and so on. Why can't the caller just call back?

My qallunaaq worked in another building. I asked her if I could phone her the next day. I discovered that it was not so scary after all, and it was rather fun to feel that I had mastered another machine. But each time, when I did learn something new, I felt a little change in me. Somehow I seemed braver and braver, but still very shy.

To Please a Friend

There were things that I was willing to try, but others I did not care for. Bicycling was one of the things I did not care for. There were things imposed on me that I could refuse, but to please a friend one day I agreed to go bicycling. We started off from Rideau Street and planned to cycle up to Sussex Drive. I got on; in that instant I had to summon all the senses that had not been used since I left home, my eyes, my ears, my sense of direction, my balance and most of all my nerves. All these things I had been taught to use in order to survive. A car screeched behind me. I looked, and all I could see was the driver shouting with a mad look on his face. And there was my friend yelling, "Minnie! Stop! Stop!" My nerves went all tense and my heart seemed to beat all over my body. My friend was right behind me, reminding me to stay on the right side, making me all the more fearful. When we finally got home, my friend was able to relax casually on her bed, while I was still shaking. And all I whispered to myself was peace, Minnie, peace, peace, peace.

Out of the Box

Television was something I could not get over. Even now, if I had the freedom to watch it day and night I would. Commercials fascinated me the most, not because of what they advertised, but because of the way they came on — everything seemed to flash quickly and disappear just as quickly, as if they didn't really want people to see what it was. It made me wonder how it happened. Where does the picture come from? How do people that are on television get inside? How do they know what to say? I found out quite by accident one black day.

A man came to me and said that I had to be televised. I was given fifteen minutes to get ready. Will I be boxed in? My imagination began to take over. My second worst enemy, other than shyness, began to work within me: I will not be able to breathe! Whenever there is no light or daylight, I feel I am being smothered.

I was told to tell the taxi driver where to go. Me? Tell him where to go? He should know where it is, he is from around here. But I relayed the instructions politely to the driver, and to my relief he did not seem to mind being told by a person who was younger than himself. Not long after I saw a sign with red lights, so pretty against the blue sky. The sign said CBC. When I entered the building everyone I saw had a beautiful smile and seemed very friendly. A man came over and shook my hand and introduced himself. His name was Percy Saltzman. He asked me questions. "What do you miss most from home? What can you not get used to here?" I was amazed by him. He was the first *qallunaaq* who asked human questions. For a long time he stood out in my memory. I told myself that somewhere in this world of the *qallunaat* lived people with sensitive minds.

The next day people kept coming to tell me that they had seen me on television. I felt shy and awkward that I was seen by so many people and that my very private thoughts were known by them all. But I stopped worrying about how television works after that. I know now that people on television are not boxed in.

I Did Not Hear Him Arrive

I had been a year in the South before I saw another Inuk. The man, just returned from Greenland, was on his way home to Cornwallis Island, Northwest Territories. I wanted to hug him. I wanted to welcome him the way I would have in my own home, to make tea and talk about his trip. But I could not. My surroundings did not allow me to be me at all. The steel desks seemed to say, you are part of us, do not act like a human being. There was a lump in my throat and my tears were hard to keep back.

I was so happy to see him, not only because he was Inuk but because he knew Inuk ways. His reawakening of the Inuit in me made me realize how alone I was. He told me about his family; he had a daughter almost the same age as me and he said that I would meet her one day. He made me wish that I had an Inuk girl to chum with, someone who saw things in the Inuit way. No matter how hard I tried to communicate with my *qallunaaq*, my comments never seemed to hit her right. He also made me realize that I was losing the sense of humour that my parents had considered so important to survival on unfamiliar ground. My "Inukism" was slowly disappearing, being buried deeper and deeper. With an effort, I tried to bring out my normal reaction to his arrival and said, "I did not hear you arrive, where did you park your dogs?" That hit him right on the Inuk funny spot and he laughed. My welcoming instincts slowly began to come back.

Grandmother's Quillik was Very Bright

I have known about electricity since I was five years old, but its power was not known to me until I saw electric lights. In school I was taught that electricity came from thunder and lightning. To me, it meant danger, and I was brought up to be very cautious of lightning and thunder at home. When there was a thunderstorm, my brother and I were always reminded to put our hands on our ears as the sound could injure the nerves inside us, even kill us. We were never allowed to handle anything shiny, such as iron or metal cans, while it stormed. We were told that such objects attracted thunder and lightning.

I learned that electricity is dangerous but also very wonderful, and useful, and I compared it to the *quillik* — the seal oil lamp, which was also wonderful, useful and a comfort to us. Every evening women would sit down on the floor or ground, catching the last speck of daylight, to clean and fix the wick of the *quillik*. Watching my grandmother, it never occurred to me that there was another such light, brighter than what I thought was so bright. To my thinking, that is what the *qallunaat* woman has as a source of comfort. Here in the South, she has light merely by flicking a most innocent looking gadget on the wall. The Inuit woman has first of all to make sure the seal oil is ready to be poured into a pot, the oil having been rendered from the fats of the seal. The wick has to be cut neatly and even, so it will not give smoke or cause any odor. The burned part of the wick has to be trimmed off, so it will give an even flame. The oil has to be poured into another pan from the original processing pan in order that the saturated parts of cooked fat may be removed. Doing this was a comfort to an Inuk woman.

Sometimes these lamps were lit early in the morning, before the sun came up, so the women could finish sewing the garments to be worn by the men that same morning. The *quillik* was her only light during the early darkness of winter. Who can say who enjoys more comfort? It is me who is comfortable today because I can reach up and switch on a gadget, because I do not have to reach down and put in all that work in order to enjoy a single flame. Though I realize how lucky I am, I will never cease to believe that my ancestors were smart and resourceful. But I do have a reason to be afraid of thunderstorms, because I can see now what it can do in the hands of the *qallunaat*. I have been told by *qallunaat* individuals that thunderstorms cannot hurt me. But I still will not stay close to shiny objects. If it storms while I am at home, I cover everything that shines.

Almost Lost an Arm for a Stamp

Sooner or later I had to write letters to my family and friends. I had known for a long time that a letter had to have a stamp in order to be mailed, but I had never quite understood what it was for. I knew neither where the stamps came from nor where to buy them. One day I found out where these little stickers were available. It was one of those days when my *qallunaaq* and I met after work; she said that she had to get stamps from the post office. I just followed her until we arrived at an enormous building.

The first thing I noticed were the odd-looking doors. I was afraid to enter through them but my *qallunaaq* did not seem bothered. I was right behind her and did not notice that when she pushed it, it began to revolve. I was so busy trying to figure out what made it go around that I forgot myself. The next thing I knew my arm was caught. A woman behind me was screaming, "She's caught!" over and over. I panicked; nothing was coming out of me but little aching sounds. By this time a crowd had gathered, and someone managed to pull the revolving door backwards. My arm was so sore that I was in tears. This made me feel all the more awkward as I was taught never to shed a tear in public. I learned two things on this occasion: that someone in pain is very exciting to people, and that this was the place where stamps came from.

I felt a bit afraid to handle the stamps I bought, and many questions began to pour into my mind. Why does a letter have to have a stamp? Is there something that has to be done to it? Not quite knowing anything about it I handled them very carefully, with high respect, as if I might break some law if I did not take care of them. The image of the Queen on the stamp also made me feel afraid, as if she would know how I was handling her. After sixteen years in the South, I know why stamps are necessary. Everything has its own place in the South, it seems.

Elevator and Escalator

On my way to work I passed many shops. I would ask myself, who goes to these shops? Can I go in too? They did not look like the Hudson's Bay stores I had known in the North. Having met many girls at the Terrace, I knew of one who enjoyed sewing as I did. She told me about shops where I could buy material to make dresses. If she can enter such shops, so can I.

Walking into a shop in the South made me want to tiptoe. So elegant! A lady came to me. "Can I help?" I had never known the freedom to select the fabric and colour I wanted. I was used to Hudson's Bay Company clerks making the choices; it did not matter the colour or size, they simply handed it to you and told you the price. Somehow I felt a little helpless making my own choice. The lady made me feel worse standing around, not saying a word after offering her help. I decided that the longer I stayed, the longer I would suffer. I chose what hit my eyes first: a wool fabric in turquoise. I went home and decided to make a jumper.

Not long after I finished the jumper, I needed something to wear underneath it. I felt nervous just thinking about the lady and about choosing. This time I was wiser and made up my mind beforehand. Off I went, this time to a big department store. Entering the store, I again had the impression of a crowd of people, each person carrying a heavy load. Some hurrying, some browsing and none enjoying this elegant store. No matter what my purpose was when I went shopping, I always forgot it when I got into the crowds. All I wanted to do was sit and watch all these people.

That's what I was doing when a lady woke me out of it. "Can I help?" I asked her where I could find a sweater. She directed me to the second floor and pointed the way. I went where she pointed. What I saw there amazed me — a crawling thing with a sign above it, ESCALATOR. Qanuk taima? — What now? I felt very far removed from the sweater I wanted, though it did not seem so important anymore. The crawling thing was now mine to master. I watched the others for awhile, especially their feet. I walked over and stepped onto the moving part; it did not feel as scary as it looked from the bottom. I kept my eyes on the feet of the person in front of me and copied. It is amazing how one can feel like one of the crowd just because one is doing something that others are doing. That's how I felt at that moment, riding on the crawling thing — pardon me — escalator.

But once I was at the other end I felt very much alone. I did not see any sign of sweaters. My greatest worry now was how to get back downstairs. I told myself to forget the sweater and started to walk around to find a way down. Not far from the escalator I read a sign: ELEVATOR. Well! I know what that is, I use it everyday at my working place. I felt like shouting at the top of my lungs, "*Taika* — there it is!" I was so relieved and went straight home to think about my adventure. Elevator and escalator. I told myself that they are related, but one goes straight up and down, and one crawls.

Something Familiar

The first farm I visited was the only place I recognized in the South. At least it was something I had read about while I was in school with the missionaries. It was the first time I did not have to follow my *qallunaaq* to find the cows, horses, pigs and chickens. I even knew where to go to gather eggs. Somehow my *qallunaaq* did not seem at all excited; she took it for granted, it was her home. My hunger to have a real home so close made me decide that I would call it my home. Of course, I did not tell my *qallunaaq* what I was thinking. We made many visits to this farm and before long I was calling her mother, "Mom."

"Mom" became very ill two years later. She ended up in a hospital. I went to visit her a couple of times, but she did not look at all like the "Mom" who used to serve me hot buns fresh out of the oven. As the tragedy of death had come my way many times, I had no doubt that I would never see her again. She died of yellow jaundice a few weeks later. I went to her funeral service and, watching her coffin being lowered into the ground, heard her last words to me: "Minnie, look after yourself."

Meeting a Grand Lady

I do not know the lady personally. I only call her a grand lady because I see her pictures in the papers so often with little children. I think any woman who takes time to see children, especially those not her own, is a grand lady. One day I was sent a notice to meet this woman. Upon arriving at her home, the Governor General's residence, I wanted to tiptoe as I often felt on entering elegant shops. I suppose I had visions that she would meet me at the door as does any other visited person. It was fascinating to find out that such grand ladies have ladies-in-waiting. I met the lady-in-waiting who took me down a long hallway. My feet never made a sound; it felt like walking on fresh-fallen snow, this hall covered with deep pile red carpet. At the end of the hall we entered a room furnished with many chairs. (It was just like arriving at Laurentian Terrace!) There stood the grand lady, Mme. Georges Vanier.

As usual, I felt shy and speechless, but she made it possible for me to be completely at ease. I was shown the greenhouse. Flowers in the middle of winter? I could not believe it. In this greenhouse were all kinds of flowers and that day I fell in love with flowers for the first time. I had always taken them for granted, as wildflowers grow all over my land, though these ones were much bigger than I was used to seeing. The grand lady gave me one which she called a chrysanthemum. I learned the names of different flowers, and I signed my own name in the visitors' book. Visitors' book? *Qallunaat* have strange visiting habits.

Dog Meat in the South?

It was one of those days when my *qallunaaq* and I met after work. She suggested that we eat at a restaurant. I had no idea just what to do there. As usual I followed my *qallunaaq* without question. A lady came over and handed us a folded sheet of paper. "Menu," it read. Do we sit here and figure out what to cook for ourselves? I felt lost; it was not at all like the place where we ate at the Terrace.

Finally I became aware of the other people in this restaurant. They were not doing anything but eating. The lady was passing food around. Ah! I have to tell the lady what I want and she will go and cook it.

I had discovered that there was nothing free in the South, so I had to think about the cost of what I was about to ask the lady to cook for me. For the first time I had a good look at the sheet of paper. There it showed the prices. Anything that sounded good was beyond the amount in my purse. Finally, my qallunaaq said that she would have a hot dog. I burst out laughing and could not stop. What is a hot dog? Do not tell me people in the South eat dog meat! I felt a bit sick. Which one is that? She pointed: wiener on a bun, twenty-five cents. I asked the lady to cook one for me as well; in fact, I asked for everything my qallunaaq asked for — cola, jello and a hot dog. When the dog was brought to our table I stared at it. I was very hungry at that moment and began to picture nice fresh seal meat, but the aroma of the dog killed it. I did not like it. I washed the taste down with cola. Unfortunately, cola became a habit of mine; I drank so much that my face broke into a million pimples!

I Hate Water

Water and beach I can understand. My qallunaaq wanted to go swimming one day and I wanted company. I did not know how to swim, but I liked the sound of the beach; it sounded familiar. Amisuaaluit! Many people! Just like a flock of geese feeding on a swamp. Some were in the water, some lying around, some walking. But they were not "together." There were couples, others in fours and others alone. It amazed me that so many people could ignore each other when they were only a few inches apart.

I do not know what I was doing at that beach, especially since I hated water. I have hated water since I was six years old. It was during springtime, in May, that my family and I were returning from goose hunting. At this time of the year at Cape Hope Island the ice on the sea is very thin. We were approaching our camp when suddenly I fell off the sled and went straight into the water, right up to my neck. I was barely holding on to the sled when our dogs stopped themselves and looked back as if they knew something was wrong. My grandmother and brother reached back quickly to pull me out. I looked down at the hole I had just come out of; it was so dark and so deep that I have never really erased it from my mind. It came back to me at this beach while I watched my qallunaaq swim without fear. I had no desire at all to try it; instead, I sat on the sand and watched people. People fascinated me so.

Square Dancing

There have been many disappointments for me since I came to the South. When my qallunaaq suggested that we go square dancing, it sounded like lots of fun. But often things that sounded like fun did not turn out the way I had expected.

We entered the dance hall and I felt excited. (Even fun was not free — it cost fifty cents to enter.) I had done square dancing at home, but never experienced it in the South. "May I have this dance?" a gentleman asked. Once more I learned something new. I was used to the men in the North who took your hand and led you to the floor. I told myself that I had come to dance, so my answer was yes. I had not thought about partners when we headed to this hall. All over again I felt shy and vowed never to go again. To this day I do not know the gentleman's name, though he had asked what part of China I was from. Who had ever heard about the North?

Twenty-one, but One Year Old in the South

I had just turned twenty-one and the people in the office where I worked gave me a cake with candles on it. We gathered in the steno pool and everybody talked and laughed to each other while I stood in front of the cake, not knowing what to say. I tried to look at each one of them and wondered how many knew that Inuit don't celebrate birthdays, that we don't reckon maturity in terms of years. And I also wondered what the reaction would be if I were to speak in that direction. Instead, I thought about the trouble they had gone to, to make my day happy. All these important people were taking the time to stand around me for this day. All I could say was thank you, and I thought to myself that I was now one year old here in the South, an anniversary which no one mentioned.

According to the office manager, I was now able to take ten days' holiday. I decided to go home and see my parents.

Arriving at my home was unforgettable. Everything looked small but familiar. It was so peaceful. Nobody was hurrying or looked like they were carrying a load. There were no red and green lights to think about while walking, no looking twice before setting out, no keys to remember on entering a tent, no meal rules to follow. Even the clock, which I looked at first thing in the morning and last thing at night, no longer seemed important.

I Thought I was a Queen

My first day at home saw a lot of handshaking. I felt very important and noticed that what I said was listened to. I attracted that kind of attention for a couple of days, at least I tried to. On the third morning, my bubble burst. My grandmother had not changed. She was still the same and most of all, still had her own rules. Her attitudes towards me and my brother remained: that we must get up as soon as we wake, dress and go out and look at the world.

According to my grandmother I was no longer a lady. She told me that my mouth had grown too much, that I was lazy and too spoiled, that I was like an icicle which would break if I was given orders. I had to join in the chores, clean the tent, get pails of water, cut wood, help my brother to look at the nets in the water, clean the fish, pluck the ducks, make bannock, do washing, heat the water on the fire — many, many things I had not done since I went to the South. When bedtime came my muscles ached and sleep was not hard to find. I became a queen again, but in a different sense. I was praised for the chores I could still perform. Our visitors were amazed that I did not forget my language and that I did not turn up my nose at my chores, that I did not ignore people, and most of all that I could still touch sealskin and eat seal meat, even raw. Nobody had the right to put me back in my place but grandmother.

Caught between Two Lives

When I left for my holidays, I was given a choice by my chief: I could stay at home, or I could come back and still have my job. But there were many complications to such a decision and four other people involved.

At the time of my birth a young man had been chosen to be my husband by my father and the mother of the young man. It was known all over our community that it was to be so. Both grandmother and grandfather had let this go on, much against their will, in order to keep peace with father and between father and the parents of the young man. I am sure that being older and wiser, they knew all the time that it was not meant to be. When I think about it myself, the relationship had never been as strong as it should be in such arrangements. I was never allowed to be alone with this man in my growing years like all the other girls in the same situation. When I sewed things he was never mentioned, nor were songs sung for me, that I would make him a good wife. It seems the whole arrangement was rather artificial. Nobody dared talk about the real reasons for this when it involved economic considerations. Customarily the agreement between the mother and my father formed a bond never to be broken, though in actual fact it could be with good reason.

The parents of this young man came from their camp when they heard that I was home from the South. There was so much tension among my family and the parents of the man. The young man himself did not come. His mother announced that he was waiting for me at the camp. In the tent sat my grandmother, acting very cold towards our visitors. She bothered to serve tea only because it was our custom, but I could see that her heart was not in it. My father also sat, looking very troubled. He knew grandmother was against the marriage, yet very fond of the parents of the man. And there was I, causing all the tension and having no say about it. Finally the mother asked, "Are we taking Minnie with us? You know she is long past the age of our promise." No one spoke. My brother and I looked at each other, he making funny faces at me. Finally grandmother spoke, but very abruptly: "Minnie has work to do; she is going back to the South." I could sense that this was not really her wish, but her way out. She had always observed that this young man was too lazy and never went hunting, and if he did he was never successful. According to her, I would have starved. She had always commented that my knowledge of caring for a home was too much for him. Nothing was said again, at least not in front of me. Altogether the whole thing appeared forgotten, but the mother never accepted it. She said later that her son would wait no longer and declared him free to marry anyone he wished. The bond was broken.

I was feeling caught between two lives when my father told me that I could stay if I wanted, or go back south. To this day I do not know how he felt. I knew that he always believed that his children should have a chance to learn different things and to meet different people. I felt very helpless and very much alone. I had to make my own choice. Suddenly, all the things I had learned about choosing on my own began to come back in my mind. I began to analyze my situation. If I stayed I would never see all the nice shops again. I would have no freedom, nor, most of all, a private life. On the other hand, I felt unwanted by my family; I told myself that they did not care about me anymore.

I went back to the South excited, but very much alone. The Terrace seemed empty. There, nobody cared what you did, but people did care in my home — about every little thing. That day I became "southernized" in my mind. I told myself that I would just have to be two people. Here in the South I mind my own affairs, make up my own mind, care for my own chores. But when I go home I have to involve myself in other chores and mind my elders. It was never true that my family did not love me or that I was unwanted by them. Today, they are most happy to have me and I enjoy my visits, as long as I remember that I have to adapt. I went back to the routine of the South and accepted it without question.

He Wrote Only a Few Words

I have learned that there are many kinds of contests in the South. A girl came to me one day and said that I should enter a Miss Northern Affairs contest. This one I just had to see and it had a challenging ring to it, so I entered. As soon as I arrived at the building where the contestants were meeting, I began to regret my decision.

There were so many people and judges and over thirty-six contestants. We each had a number; mine was seven. We stood in a line-up. When the first number was called my heart pounded. I could see what the first girl was doing. I just could not walk like that, nor could I smile on my own. For the first time since I came south I asked myself, "what am I doing here?" I had gone too far. The sound of clapping hands came from the other room. By then I was shaking. When I heard my number called, my mind argued with itself. I have to go . . . I have gone too far . . . this is no time to be shy . . . I see most of these people every time I go to work. . . . Out I went. My smile was no problem, a smile can hide many kinds of fears. I could not help smiling at all those people — but I was so glad it was all over. I was told that I would have to wait until all the others had done the same. I waited and my number was called again. This time there were only seven of us. I was told that I had to do it a third time! When it was over I had come second to Miss Northern Affairs.

What does one do, to come second to a queen? I met a photographer and a man who wrote only a few words. I had never seen anyone who took pictures like that. The photographer worked hurriedly and he kept putting some little gadget near my face and he clicked just as fast. In the meantime another man was writing while he asked questions, but he wrote very little. I told myself that he must be careless. My *qallunaaq* had come to the contest and could not wait for the paper to come out. As usual, I did not know what she was talking about. I met my *qallunaaq* after work and we went straight to the newspaper stand. We found a bench on our way home and began to read: "ESKIMO GIRL SECOND IN CS BEAUTY CONTEST. Minnie Oadla, 29, of Old Factory, became possibly the first Eskimo woman to place in a beauty contest with white women here today." It went on and on, where I came from and what I liked. My *qallunaaq* was horrified by the mistake in my age and told me that I should get them to correct it. I could not be bothered about that. I had had enough for one day. But it was no wonder the writer had made mistakes — he wrote only a few words. He had even misspelled my last name.

My Feelings were Hurt

How did I allow myself to get into the things I did? I never understood until I was in the middle of them. I found myself one day in a building with a lot of big cameras, wires dangling down from the ceiling and a man walking around with a great big machine. A lady took me to a room of mirrors and began to paint my face. My skin felt gooey, sticky and stiff. The lady called it make-up. Then I was made to put on a parka in the middle of July, when the temperature outside was eighty degrees. It would not have been so bad inside the building, but up I went, right to the roof, where the sun beamed down. A man made a movie of me while I drank ginger ale. I understood that I was advertising the ginger ale.

Seeing my picture on the back of Pure Spring Ginger Ale trucks made me feel uneasy. My feelings were hurt, especially when girls I knew would come to me and say, "Who do you think you are? Why did they pick you? Why does it have to be an Eskimo?" I began to notice that some I considered to be friends would not have anything to do with me, and that others seemed to be proud just to know me. I decided that I would rather keep my friends than have my picture behind a truck, so I refused the next time I was asked to advertise. The man who talked to me about it told me that I should do it to make extra money. I started to cry; it seemed he did not care for my feelings. He repeated that it was up to me, so I refused. He said that I was odd, that other girls were just itching to be televised, that I should be proud to be chosen. To this day the man does not know that I had to put up with insults and angry letters. How can people waste time and stamps to send such letters?

Visiting a Mint

What is a mint? The only kind of mint I knew was a candy flavour. One day my *qallunaaq* said, "Let's go see the Mint today, it's on our street and not very far from here." We walked to the Mint and on approaching I felt a little afraid. There was an RCMP standing at the gate. The building was surrounded by many harpoons, or so it seemed to my Inuk eyes. I learned later that it was just a steel fence. Inside the fence stood the smallest house I had ever seen. Who could live in there? There was another policeman inside. He handed each of us a piece of paper with a number on it. Oh, no! Don't tell me I have to stand in front of many people again. I followed my *qallunaaq*. We went through a hallway and could hear a lot of noise, a lot of machines running. Money, money — I have never seen so many pennies. We went closer. There were many machines going, one sideways, another up and down. At one end it ate blocks of copper-coloured stones; at the other end, it vomited pennies. So this was where money was made. Mint? Well, that is another mystery for me.

We were Nomads

I had never heard about the West. I had learned my geography by provinces, though I had never really understood what they meant. Whoever heard of places that are divided up when they are so close together? Not me.

My work as a translator took me to the West one summer, along with a welfare worker. We travelled by airplane — a house in the air. Our first stop was Fort William, Ontario, where we were to change planes. How did my companion know what to do? When we got off the airplane she knew where to go. I just followed. She seemed to know my mind and from then on she began to tell me many things. She showed me how to check my air ticket, how to find my luggage, how to find out the departure and arrival times, where the book stands were, where the lavatory was, and why the people stood behind counters.

We took another airplane and arrived at Edmonton. We were to stay at a hotel. She showed me how to check in. I was so surprised to find my name written on a card in this hotel — I had never been here, how did they know my name? I asked her about it since she was so willing to tell me things. She said that she had booked it. Booked it? The English language becomes funnier everyday. She said that she telephoned this hotel. Magic, these *qallunaat* ways! We were both given keys. That was something I had become used to, having keys. Once in our room, I headed for the window. *Aukataguluapingani!* Incredible, fantastic! The houses and cars and people I could see looked so tiny. But the sky still looked pretty high. Everything in the room was very elegant. It even had a television, a telephone and its own lavatory. It seemed that my companion had made all kinds of arrangements before we ever got there.

The purpose of our trip was to visit patients in hospitals and homes who served the Inuit. The next day we went to Charles Camsell Hospital. It was very sad to see all these Inuit. Some had children in the North from whom they had not heard since they arrived. So many worries and yet they were just like me, accepting their surroundings without question. I felt a bit useless in my job because I had never heard the Inuit language of the western Arctic. I tried to speak with some but could not understand. They didn't understand when I spoke to them and yet they seemed so happy to see me. All I could do was return my Inuk smile to let them know that I felt for them.

We then moved on to Clearwater Lake, Manitoba. We travelled in a bush plane which was familiar to me, but I had never had such a trip. Flying over mountains, we bounced up and down and I felt very afraid. When we arrived, we both felt quite lost. My companion had made arrangements for somebody to pick us up, but they did not appear. She telephoned, and not long after a doctor came and took us to a hotel. We seemed to have gone from one extreme to another. In Edmonton we had stayed in an elegant hotel and our luggage had been carried for us. Here we could only laugh at our situation. We checked in. The man behind the counter did not seem to care whether we stayed or not. He was not in a hurry. It seemed he had no time to watch or rules to go by, which made him seem like an odd qallunaaq to me. My companion asked about our luggage; the man told us that we had to carry them ourselves. I did not care since I have carried heavier loads than my suitcases before. There was no elevator. I followed my companion. With her suitcases in her hands, along with her coat, camera and purse, she took hold of the bannister and started to climb the stairs. When she stepped up, the bannister almost came off in her hand!

We entered our room and I went to the window; on moving the curtain, dust flew around me. I looked out and saw old papers lying about on untended lawns. It was dead looking. My companion and I just sat for a while; we were tired, mostly from laughing so much. I could tell that I had not had a good laugh for a long time because the muscles in my stomach were aching. The floors in the room were all bumpy and there was no carpet. It did not bother us; after all, we were nomads.

The Fish Like to be Dressed For

Our stay in Clearwater fell on a weekend. Those who we hoped to see were not in town. It was on the Saturday that one of the doctors asked if we would like to go fishing. I was all for it; fishing I have known since I was very little. We travelled quite a way by car to a lake. There was me, in a pink suit and high-heel shoes, catching fish by the dozen while my companions were not getting any.

They were dressed for it in jeans and old shirts and flat shoes. Who thought that I would get a chance to go fishing while visiting hospitals? I had no such clothing with me, so I went in my suit and best shoes. My companions began to joke and tease me that maybe the fish liked to be dressed up for.

Hospital Visits

Our next stop was Brandon, Manitoba. By this time I realized that there were many Inuit in the hospitals. I felt very sad, knowing what they were missing and what worried them. Most of these patients were mothers and fathers. How were their homes managing with all the work that had to be done, especially the provision of food and clothing? Some had been in hospital for two years, some for one year and others for six months. Some had heard nothing of their relatives for a long time. Some did, and had had bad news about loved ones who had died. I wished that I could take their places so that they might go home and enjoy their families. The job I was doing was not very pleasant for me.

We then went to St. Boniface, Manitoba. We saw a child there who had forgotten his language completely. This was as sad as any illness. How will he communicate with his parents when he goes home? My companion was a very understanding lady. She seemed to know what made me unhappy and always brought me out of it. When she was not busy with her writing, phoning and arrangements, she took time to tell me a lot of little things. She even taught me how to handle a knife and fork while eating properly, as she called it.

Our next visit was to a hostel. There we met people who were waiting to go home. The house reminded me of the hotel in Clearwater Lake. It was even worse because it had the smell of a human who has not washed for years. The Inuit looked as if they had not been out for months. They were so pale, not like the skin I am used to seeing on Inuit — wind-burned and sun-tanned. Their lavatory was horribly messy, dirty and smelly. And these were the people who were waiting to go home after hospital care. It would be no wonder if they went right back to the hospital. The lady who had opened the door for us did not seem to care at all. She wore a low-necked black blouse, her hair had black roots and on top was dried and blonde. She looked like she had two big red apples on both sides of her nose and her lips were smeared with the same red colour. She fascinated me in a funny sort of way and I wondered why people take the time to ruin themselves. I do not know which appalled us most — the smelly upstairs or the lady downstairs. I was taught not to make comments on anything I saw or heard as long as I was with anyone older than myself, so I remained silent. But it was obvious that my companion did not like what she saw either, and she wasted no time in going back to the hospital and telling the doctor about it. Perhaps the people in the hospitals were not so badly off; at least they were in good care.

It had been a month since my companion and I left Ottawa; finally we headed back. It seemed everytime I returned from a trip, my adopted home became sweeter and warmer. Even my *qallunaaq* seemed larger than life and so good to see when I came back.

Some months later we visited hospitals in Quebec. It was much different from what I had experienced in the West. The patients looked so much happier and were well-informed about why they were in hospital. Some even knew the date when they would go home. But the things that saddened me just seemed to get worse. I had never visited a mental hospital, though I had looked after a mentally sick man. This was to be my first visit to such a hospital. The building itself was standing inside a steel fence, like the Mint. It looked so empty inside and every door had bars. The Inuk man we were to visit happened to be my cousin, one of my uncle's sons. I had seen him last at Moosonee Hospital and at that time he was waiting to go home. My father had written later that he was home and then wrote again that he was back in the hospital. Apparently he had serious mental worries.

I wished that crying was not so embarrassing in front of people. I could hardly hold on to my tears when I saw this man amongst men who did not seem to notice anything and who looked at me with blank faces. When I spoke to him he seemed to remember; in fact, he asked who I was and I told him. He repeated my name as if he knew it. I felt so much pain, knowing that his mother was dead and that all his sisters were grown up and married and having their own children. I especially felt sad because I knew the reasons for his mental illness. Our Inuit beliefs as to why he was sick were well-known at home. We believed that people can become emotionally sick from severe treatment and *qiilingunik*, sadism. There was another Inuk man, about his age, who used to enjoy teasing him and playing tricks on him. This man played terrible tricks, like putting traps in his bed. He scared him while in a canoe on their travels. He dressed up in a horrible face with soot on very dark nights. He made up stories that he was having affairs with his sisters. This was an endless torment and the victim became ill as a result. Today the villain is an outcast, and there is no greater punishment than to be ignored by the whole community. My cousin is now home with what is left of his family. But how sad that his life was ruined by another man who was a lot sicker than he at the beginning.

My Frustration

During my childhood I knew only three eating utensils — plate, cup and *ulu*, a knife that belongs only to a female. Its blade is shaped like a half moon and it has a good gripping handle. It can be sharp as a razor blade. This knife is very·important to an Inuk woman; according to our traditions one has·to be a female to own one. Though I have learned in school what knives, forks and spoons are, I owned an *ulu* at home. Nobody used it but me, as every woman has one of her own. It is only with this that I ate, along with my hands and teeth. I have become used to knives, forks and spoons but there were times when I longed to eat naturally.

I learned about different kinds of food while living at the Terrace. Everyday there was a menu posted at the door of our dining hall. By the time I had been there a year I had learned the names of the foods. Sometimes we would have spareribs and chicken legs. I used to get the urge to eat my own way, to pick them up with my hands and really enjoy them. My surroundings would not let me. Only Henry the Eighth seemed to have been allowed to do it in public. I felt too shy. If I did, I would have to get up and go wash my hands, and by the time I got back to my table my tray would be gone. It was very frustrating not being able to eat with my hands.

Just Close Your Eyes and Eat

Having been to one restaurant, I thought they were all the same. But I have learned there are many kinds. Once my *qallunaaq* and I decided not to take our lunch at our residence but to have lunch in a restaurant. When I met her she said, "Let's have some Chinese food." I had no idea what Chinese food was. I have met Chinese people; in fact, I have been taken for one so often that I was beginning to think that I knew them.

The place we entered looked very colourful. In one corner were two doors with something written on them. It looked like someone had thrown black paint at the doors and the results were these funny shapes. We were given a menu. As usual my *qallunaaq* was completely oblivious to my confusion, so I simply followed her. I ordered what she ordered. That is Chinese food? It looked like the stew my grandmother made for pups. "I have not had any for ages," my *qallunaaq* said. If she had had it before, it must be edible. I will eat it. Scooping it up, something seemed to rise in my throat. When finally I found the courage to eat it, the taste was not so sickening as expected. It took me some time to like this *alurassak*, this prepared dog food, but today I am crazy about it and call it by its respected name — Chinese Food. I even look at it while eating.

Goose Pimples All Over

By this time, after about a year, I had met many people. One of them asked me if I would like to go to the museum. Where is that? What is that? I followed the lady.

When we arrived, the huge doors of the building made me feel tiny. I could not believe that they actually opened. (Strange that nobody met us; I was getting used to being met at the door. One cannot just walk into any house like I do at home.) We began to walk around. It did not look like a store or any other building I had been in. The lady seemed to know everything. As we went on, some of the things I saw were strange, others looked familiar. Everything looked so old. They must be *pimmarriaaluit*, treasured. The lady went on and on, telling me that these animals lived in Alberta at one time. Alberta? I have been there and it's not so far. I decided that this building is where the *qallunaat* gather old things. Yes, it must be old things; even Inuit do not have boats like that today. Yet some of the animals I saw still existed where I came from. I felt very confused. Looking at all these big animal bones I began to picture them alive. All over me came goose pimples.

Life or Death

One day I decided to go for a walk on my own. I told myself not to think about the clock or my stomach. If I became hungry I would go to a restaurant. The street on which I walked became bare, no buildings anywhere. I felt a sudden release. In fact, I felt I was coming out of a tent, and there was nothing there to crush me. There were trees and nice grass that was evenly cut. I could not believe that it grew so neatly. It felt so quiet and I felt so free that I wanted to run and jump all over. I had not realized how much I missed the peace with nature that I knew at home. My whole body began to relax.

Suddenly, out of nowhere, someone was screaming, "Hey, you!" I looked around and there was a man coming towards me. He looked like a policeman. My heart was jumping all over my body, my knees were weak. I did not know what was going to happen or what he was going to do to me. He asked if I did not know or read English; I said I did. I guess I was so happy in my freedom that I failed to notice a little sign that read "Keep off the grass." I had just passed it by like a piece of stone or twig. I said that I was sorry, that I did not see it. He became very understanding and told me not to let it happen again.

On my way back, I talked to myself all the way. *Qallunaat* are *sunatuinnangitualluit*, particular. The whole thing was crazy to me. *Atummaqai?* I suppose it is necessary? The man made it sound so important and had been so worked up about walking on the grass. It made me wonder what *qallunaat* do when it's very important. I have never seen a man at home who got all worked up unless it was a matter of life or death. I did not see that I endangered anything. Who is free? Not I, as long as I lived in the South.

I Have Seen Many Deaths

I have seen many deaths, and have kissed many dead people before they were buried, ever since I was a child. Our tradition for the dead has always been to mourn for one year. The graves of close dead relatives must be visited often. The family of the dead has to wear black clothes for a year. If one wears bright clothes, one has to have a black strip around the sleeve of the garment. Our belief is that no one really dies until someone is named after the dead person. So, to leave the dead in peace and to prevent their spirits from being scattered all over the community, we give their names to the newborn. Not until then do we believe that the dead person is spiritually in his grave. The minds of the people do not rest until the dead have been renamed. It is like leaving the dead dispossessed and deprived of their rightful rest.

I had never really stopped to think about death. I accepted it like any of the other losses we experience in the North. I guess the ritual we followed was created for that reason, so that we would not think about death itself. For one year the close relatives cannot go to festive activities or dances, nor are they allowed to make jokes. I had never actually realized that death meant a loss of life, even though our ritual demanded that we touch the dead before burial, to make us understand that the person will no longer respond.

I had come to know a man who worked with me. He told me about many Inuit who live in parts of the North other than my own. He had shown me maps of the world. He also spoke my language and used Inuk manners when he approached me. It was he who drove me to the Terrace when I first arrived in Ottawa in 1957. When one feels very alone, one always finds some reason or other to depend on someone either physically, mentally or for moral support. That was how I was beginning to feel about this man. It was because of him that my work was meaningful. It was because of him that I struggled in this strange *qallunaat* world. Now he is dead. His death was the first I understood: he was gone forever, never to be seen again. I went to see him at the funeral home, and the building itself made me feel sad. I had kissed and touched many dead relatives, but my surroundings would not let me follow the ritual I was brought up to observe. Looking at him in the casket, in the suit which I had often seen him wearing while walking, sitting and talking and responding, it suddenly hit me that he would never do those things again. My eyes were aching but I had not one tear. I wanted to get out and be on my own; I wanted no one to touch me or talk to me. I thought about my mother, who had died when I was three years old; I thought about my grandmother, on my mother's side, who died when I was ten; I thought about my grandfather, who died when I was sixteen. I thought about all my little cousins, who died during a measles epidemic at home. This man had taught me about the maps of the world and he had taught me the sense of loss in death.

I Am in the Middle

In 1958 my job as a translator took me to Frobisher Bay, Baffin Island, Northwest Territories. Because I was a working girl, I lived with a *qallunaaq* woman. Our conversations were simple: good morning and good night. Because I was from somewhere else the Inuit were strange to me and I was strange to them. The *qallunaat* with whom I worked accepted me from 9:00 A.M. to 5:00 P.M.; socially, I did not exist. I was friends with the *qallunaat* as long as I made parkas and translated for them. I should have been sad all the time but I was too busy studying the people around me. Inuit were in the middle as well, like I was.

The Inuk man was caught between his desire to go hunting and the demands of the clock. He would be late for his job and get fired. His mark became unreliable so he would go hunting and feed his wife and children on the seal which he had luck with. Eventually the weather would not allow him to go hunting again or the money that was left from his last pay was all spent on ammunition and grub. But there was always an answer for him — he went on relief for a few months and tried hunting again. If he was successful with his hunting, the strong beliefs of his tradition to share with his neighbours would not allow him to eat alone with his family.

He begins to visit his friends and relatives which he has not seen since he started working like the *qallunaat*, and somehow he borrows money. In the meantime problems and worries are swelling up in his mind. His wife no longer looks up to him with happiness, she is too wrapped up herself with the problems that have arisen in her home. She is doing a lot of visiting herself, trying to get food for her children. The husband finds some friends who are making homebrew or friends who have bought from the *qallunaat*, at five to ten dollars, a bottle. He finds this drink very intriguing and it makes him forget his problems. So now he sleeps in the day and gets up at night when his friends are available.

Then one night someone in the group remembers a card game, a game which his ancestors learned from some explorer or

Hudson's Bay man. Instead of playing it just as a game to pass time, as it was played by his ancestors, he turns it into a gambling game and now money is involved. He manages to win now and then and when he does he buys all the ingredients to make homebrew. He then becomes very popular with others who are in the same situation. His home begins to be their regular meeting hall. His wife, usually terrified of people who drink, is no longer amused by her regular visitors. The rules that were given to her by the qallunaat to have the children in school are no longer an obstacle. She has a greater obstacle to overcome, her drinking husband.

The children no longer listen to her words. They realize that the language they have learned is much stronger and has more impact. They can tell her to be quiet and to shut up. She feels very tired; she does not get enough to eat; she loses a great deal of sleep and can hardly keep awake during the day while her younger children are running around, going in and out without proper clothing. Then one day a mysterious machine of the qallunaat comes around, the ajjiliurrutik machine for taking pictures, X-ray. Not very long after she is told that she has to go south to the hospital. She does not know for how long or why; she guesses that she has tuberculosis, one of many gifts her ancestors have received from the qallunaat. She no longer sees her former problems but worries about them while in the southern hospital. Her children are now under the care of their grandparents. They can no longer answer back and find their grandparents are much stronger willed. Now they are having to grow up a different way.

Because all kinds of people fascinate me I also studied the qallunaat in the North. They are also in the middle, between their jobs in the North and their authorities in the South. In the North they appear knowledgeable in everything. They give out rules that they understand. When asked a question by the Inuit, their favourite replies are "maybe" and "will write to South." In the South, the ones receiving the letter remember the occasion when they had visited that community. To them the Inuit did not seem to have that problem. They remember their smiles and hand-shakes and recall that the schools, offices and recreation affairs looked very well at that hour of their visit. Their *siallaat*, servants, had followed their orders. Everything was working according to plan.

The letter has quite a trip itself. It has been in the hands of the receiver, receiver's head, head of the head and finally third head's head. Everybody now has something to do. The letter even went through a machine and was made into several copies. It has been some months since the letter arrived. By this time the Inuk who had asked the question will have sorted it out himself. A reply is sent finally to the original writer, telling the Inuk that those in the South will write to the people who have something to do with the question. Inuk again sits and waits; to him it sounds as if they are doing something about his problem.

Perhaps his question becomes very pressing in his mind and he decides to write himself. His letter goes to one of the heads, the head sends it to the head of the translators. The translator head sends it to the translator. The translator is very upset on reading the letter. The translator then puts the letter into English; somehow, it does not sound as pressing as it does in Inuttitut. Altogether it does not sound very important to the receiver because we translators lack many important words in English, though we know them in the Inuit language. "*Qittungara anniakuvimmut aullalaursimajuk suli tusangilara naningimaat tusarumavunga iqaumainarakku isumaalugillugo . . .*" "My child is gone to the hospital, I have not heard where he is. I would like to hear." I am still learning many things, but I have learned that the *qallunaat* language can be just as pressing as the Inuit language. "Some time ago my child was hospitalized, but I have not yet heard of his whereabouts. I would be pleased to hear as I worry about him a great deal. My mind does not rest from worry."

One day the *qallunaaq* in the North decides to go with the hunter and his dog team. On the whole, he enjoys it, enjoys the freedom of not having to watch the clock. He observes igloo building, the use of harpoons, stalking of seals, dogs being harnessed, the whip being handled. He sees how an Inuk can handle dogs with few commands, how an Inuk can get out of the ice when stuck with his sled. He does not really care for the coffee breaks; it takes too long to be made and when he finally gets it, it is full of *piluit*, caribou hairs, which fall off the outfit he is wearing. What can he do? By the time he picks them out of his cup, the coffee will be too cold to enjoy. He has to gulp it down like an Inuk.

For the first time he sees the Inuk as a capable person. In fact, he is amazed by what the Inuk can put up with. He begins to invite him to his home. While talking with him, he begins to find out a lot of things about how the Inuk lives. He begins to understand the full meaning of his language. He asks him to carve for him; the carving has a meaning itself and the Inuk explains it. He realizes for the first time that the carving speaks like the art work in the South. Bit by bit, he begins to collect. He begins to send carvings as gifts to his relatives in the South. At the same time he realizes that his job no longer deals with "just Inuit." To him the Inuit are human after all, with feelings, able to think, capable of a life which he himself would never choose. His way of approaching the Inuk begins to change; he no longer talks fast, but explains in a way that the Inuk will understand. Even his manner is no longer stiff. It has become thawed, warm, and the Inuk sees he too is human after all.

In the South, the *qallunaaq* is very friendly, he no longer walks as if he is carrying a heavy load. Sitting with his colleagues, he listens to their plans for the North. There will be a new runway for aircraft, a new school building, a new administration building, new quarters for the *qallunaat* who are employed there, a new home economist to teach the Inuit how to be clean and to show them how to wash and prepare meals, new ways to bring the Inuit children in to the school, new community affairs, a survival course for the new *qallunaat* who are to go north. There is no mention of a new way to teach Inuit how to cope with their changing lives, how to cope with liquor, how to cope with a working husband, how to plan their spending now that he is no longer a hunter.

So many things the *qallunaat* have introduced to the simple Inuk. The *qallunaaq* man feels withdrawn after listening to his boss's big plans. He wonders if his boss will understand him if he makes any comments on how to cope with the Inuit. He becomes very quiet and cannot bring himself to explain the things he has seen happen when other new ways of the South have been tried in the old North. What he says will affect his job which he cannot afford to lose. He lets his colleagues and boss dream on with their plans, and he agrees to them. He is trained to respect his superiors; what they say is always right, what they say has to be the way. No matter how he feels and how much he understands the Inuk way, he chooses to be quiet and to sit back and listen. He is now Inuit.

Being in the middle I also studied the young women in the North. At one time it was the Inuit tradition that a young woman's parents chose her husband at the earliest age. Early marriages prevented promiscuity. Now she is also in the middle, between the Inuk man and the qallunaaq man. In her changing community she has seen qallunaat women who are attired in pretty frocks and wear make-up. In her eyes they choose what they want, eat what they want, speak loudly at husbands, ditch and pick up husbands. She finds that the qallunaaq man is friendly towards her; in fact, he notices her looks and tells her so. On the other hand, the Inuk man would notice what she can do and not what she looks like. But the qallunaaq man speaks loud and makes it all so exciting for her. He arranges some meeting place where there will be more privacy. He then invites her and gives her a drink. He gives her more than he takes. Everything he says is now agreeable to her.

The meetings go on and on, until she is discovered by the police. The qallunaaq man knew the rules all the time — that he was not supposed to mingle with Inuit girls at that place. Somehow he gets out of it, in spite of the promise he made when he signed his contract to work there. The girl is now in the hands of the police. She is asked many questions. "How did you get in there? Where did you get the drink? You are not supposed to go there! What is the name of the man you were with? Who does he work for?" She knows that she will suffer a great deal more if she tells on him. She is warned not to go there again, not to drink or she will go to jail. It makes her afraid, but more so of the qallunaaq man whom she is afraid to report.

Then one day she has funny pains and an uncontrollable itch; she now carries one of his gifts — venereal disease — so now she has to go back and forth to the dispensary and take many needles to cure it. If she has not received that gift, she may find herself pregnant. Now the community sees her condition; she is suffering in her mind and it affects her family. The Inuk man whom she had rejected, rejects her for carrying a qallunaaq child. The qallunaaq man has disappeared, or if he sees her, he avoids her and acts as if he had never been intimate with her. She has to carry her problem alone. After the birth her parents become understanding again; they have gained a grandchild and they know the child did not ask to be born on its own. They also know that the new mother has paid enough for her promiscuity. Not all young women suffer this experience; yet I watched it happen, being in the middle, in my one-year stay in this community. And, of course, it does not happen only in that community; it has happened in the four corners of the world.

"Life-or-Death" Had a Reason

Back in the South in 1959, my qallunaaq and I decided to go and see a tulip show one day. I had never seen so many tulips in so many colours, nor so many people among the flowers. My weakness for watching people pulled me away from my qallunaaq. There were people taking pictures, bending down to smell the tulips. Then I saw someone who looked familiar; it was not the same man, but the uniform was the same as the one worn by the man who had got all worked up when I had walked on the grass that day. I decided that his reason must have been this, to make the grass grow for tulip shows. Why did he not tell me that? Really, qallunaat have many laws which they have no time to explain to a little Inuk like me.

Language was Pulling

I went to visit a cousin who lived in Quebec City. I had taken a train which made many stops. Along the way the names of the towns began to change to French names. Having attended a French convent school, I could understand some of the signs I saw. At each stop the train became heavier with people who spoke only French. I felt that I was the only person who spoke a strange language. During my visit, my cousin took me to many places and everywhere we went the people spoke French. Even in the shops, cashiers said, "Oui?" After two days I began to feel that there was a cellophane shield all around me. I could see the people, I could hear them and yet their words were unreachable.

On my third day I was on my way to catch a bus to visit the citadel. Among the crowd I heard a welcome voice. It sounded strange because I was hearing other voices that were not the same. The couple I could hear seemed to me like the voices of snow geese amongst many voices of Canada geese. Their words were familiar and yet odd among the others I was hearing. Their sound fascinated me and yet the language they spoke was the language I was used to hearing, English. I just kept my pace with them because their sound was comforting; I was not the only one who spoke an odd language. Their voices pulled at me and I forgot my own destination. Without being aware, I was following this couple and they were going somewhere else. I asked myself: *suruaaluvit*? What is wrong with you? I had to turn around and find my bus stop all over again.

Silly Cry

My *qallunaaq* and I celebrated our birthdays on the same date. In our first year as roommates we gave ourselves a party. By this time she and I could talk to each other about our problems, sorrows, wishes and dreams and share our female to female secrets. We got along very well, mainly because I did not argue or disagree with her suggestions or plans. I went along with everything she did and enjoyed it as well.

Someone had given me a pair of baby-doll pyjamas for my birthday. They were the new fad that year. Every girl was daring to wear them. They were beautiful. Because I was brought up by my grandmother, I inherited some of her idiosyncracies. She treasured anything that she thought was beautiful, no matter what it was. When I got into her trunk or suitcase, I would find a single necklace bead, a broken ironstone plate with flower prints on it, an old dress she picked up from her neighbours, a brand new ashtray with scenes on it, a slip that she had put away because it was too pretty to wear. So it was with these baby-doll pyjamas. I kept them in a drawer among other things that I treasured. They were very pretty to me and too pretty to wear. My other reason for not wearing them was because of my shyness.

My qallunaaq and I shared one dresser and one closet. She used one side and I, the other. Every time one of us opened our drawers we saw the other's things. Both of us knew about everything we owned. She went to bed in baby-dolls and I went to bed in my long-legged flannelette pyjamas. Neither of us really noticed or mentioned to the other what we wore to bed. It was something that was not important, so we took it for granted as one of our habits. But one evening, while she was sitting at the dresser attired in her baby-dolls, combing her hair and looking in her mirror, I opened the drawer where I kept my treasures. Whatever I needed at that moment was not in that drawer. Seeing my baby-dolls, she remembered that I had never worn them. "Do you not like those? How come you have never worn them? They are too beautiful, just to leave them in a drawer. Are they too big? Are they too small? Why don't you try them on?" What could I say to all her questions? She would not understand my reasons and besides, they were not important. I followed her suggestion. I knew that if I argued my side she would become all worked up, so I tried them on.

I felt very naked, very flashy. She became excited just the same: "Oh, how beautiful! The colour just suits you! You look so cute in them! I don't think you appreciate the girl who gave them to you! I think it's terrible to leave them in the drawer! Why don't you wear them? Are you shy? I would give anything to have nice brown skin like yours! Are you shy about your legs? Look at my legs, and I wear baby-dolls!" I began to cry. "How silly of you to cry, it's so stupid! Whoever heard of crying over baby-dolls?"

We both became very quiet. How could I explain that I did not cry over the baby-dolls? I wanted to tell her my feelings but I could not. I wanted to tell her that I treasured them because they were too pretty to wear in an old bed, that I was afraid that they might get all wrinkled, and that I did not want to wash them for fear they would lose their prettiness. I wanted to tell her that I appreciated the person who gave them to me very much and that I showed my appreciation by trying to make them last as long as possible. I wanted to tell her that I was not brought up to show off my body, that showing off the body where I come from is described as *anguniattuk*, fishing for a man, the word also used for dogs who are in heat. Where I come from, a lady does not show off what she has.

My *qallunaaq* finally broke the silence by saying, "I did not realize you were so shy. I did not mean to hurt you. I am awfully sorry. You don't have to wear them if you don't want to. After all they are yours." I wished she would just keep quiet about the whole thing. I cried because she gave me too much notice and she insulted my baby-dolls for not understanding that they were my treasures. That was the first time my *qallunaaq* and I had had unhappy feelings since we met. It was the first time I stood up for my beliefs without following hers. It made me wonder how many times we would have had unhappy feelings if I had not followed her and if instead I tried to explain my beliefs to her.

Gifts to Take North

Sometime later I asked my *qallunaaq* if she would like to come home with me during our summer holidays. She was very excited and wanted to come very much. Her first question was, "how much is the fare?" The figure appalled her, and she said that she would have to save and save. We both had six months to save for our fares and to buy all sorts of items. Her list included new clothes, a new purse, a new suitcase and a camera. My list consisted of presents for my family — fabric for both grandmother and my stepmother, guitar strings for my brother, wool to make socks for my father, baby powder for my new baby sister. I wanted to tell my qallunaaq that she did not need all those new things, but the memory of our unhappy feelings made me hesitate. I imagined her getting all worked up if I told her that she would need only what is suitable for my home — rubber boots in case we have to walk on wet grass or travel by canoe. I cannot tell her that she will need low-heeled shoes; that it would be better to bring slacks instead of a dress so that she, being a qallunaaq, would be warm; that she will need a comfortable, warm jacket; that we can share a suitcase, hers being old does not matter at all. Camera? Well, that is her qallunaaq way, to take pictures. It goes with her traditions. I wanted to tell her to take what she usually takes when we go to her farm home, but I dreaded our unhappy feelings if I tried to explain to her. I kept my mouth shut.

I decided to give fabrics to grandmother and stepmother, knowing that there is not much choice in the store where they are. I bought guitar strings for my brother because he had written to ask for some; there were no such items in the northern store. And I bought my baby sister powder because I thought it would be easier for my stepmother. Where I come from, mothers usually have to gather rotting wood, wood that is at the point of breaking like powder when squeezed with the fingers. It has to be kept near heat in order to dry. When it is flaked, one has to look for the old roots and take them out. Sometimes mothers will wrap this rotten wood in a cloth and hammer it against two stones. Again, one has to look for the roots so the baby will not get splinters. In the winter, when everything is covered with snow, it is not easily available; if it is, it is wet and takes longer to dry. Mothers then have to use soot from the woodstove. It also has to be flaked into powder but mothers don't care for it as much, as it is messier. For this reason I brought my baby sister baby powder, and I hoped it would save my stepmother all this effort.

Second Look

I often wonder why people look at me twice and almost always from the top of my head to the bottom of my feet. I could ask a few questions about it. Maybe what I am wearing seems to people to be out of place, because I am wearing *qallunaat* clothing when I look like I come from somewhere else. I have been taken for many nationalities. Some people ask, "what are you?" Some try to guess. Some take a long time to come around to the question. Some open up a subject about their world travel and talk on and on about China. At one time their questions got out of hand. They asked me what I thought of the Vietnam war. I did not know what to say about this because I had never known war. The only enemy we have in the North is the bitter cold winter or some summer weather, which can suddenly turn on us and prevent our fathers from hunting. The Vietnam war made me wonder for what reasons the people were fighting and what about? I thought about the families who were involved, little children who did not understand why their mothers and fathers were suddenly gone, the fear and suspense that was involved. Maybe that's why people give me a second look, wondering why I am not in my country when it is at war. Whoever heard of Inuk in the South anyway? Not the people I meet.

Inuit in the South

I did not know of any other government department, other than the Department of Indian Affairs and Northern Development, which brought Inuit to the South. I knew only that there was not much done for them, for their comfort. The department has programs for *qallunaat* employees who are to go north; they call it a survival course. In this program the *qallunaat* are taught how to build igloos, how to meet the hazards of the cold and some Inuit language. Everything is done, through the department, for their comfort while living in the settlements of the North. Houses are made available. The *qallunaaq* does not have to live far from wherever his job is to be. His food is taken care of before he gets there. His house is usually equipped with a washing machine, running water, a refrigerator, a stove and furniture. Besides his salary, he receives a northern allowance. In the building where he works he has a telephone, along with a list of the people he can call on. All the comforts he has known all his life are there. The only things that are strange to him are the faces of the Inuit. I have met people over and over who are amazed that the Inuit have survived in the North and so far the qallunaat have survived it as well, thanks to the precautions taken on their behalf.

I do not know of anything that has been done for the comfort of the Inuit in the South. The department has taken families out of the North to employ as translators. Before coming out, the family had no training whatsoever or any kind of preparation on how to survive in the South — though they do not forget to tell the Inuit what time to come in to work, where to sign their names in their black books and how to fill out an income tax form. There are no homes made available to couples who have children. There is no program for them to follow to find out where, how and what kind of living quarters are suitable, where and how to shop for groceries, what kind of entertainment is available to them, where to go when one of them becomes ill. They are expected to know all this for themselves as soon as they step off the plane.

The department is anxious to tell the Inuit how to clean their houses, so that the houses won't wear out so fast. I have never forgotten a speech that was made by one of the heads of the department when he arrived at the settlement. The Inuit had expected to hear something fantastic since he had come such a long way to talk especially to them. The speech went something like this: "I am very glad to be here and enjoyed my visit to your homes. I am very pleased to see that they are so clean." One old woman came over to me and asked if he was really the head of the department, and if so, why he did not have the intelligence to tell us something important, instead of telling us what our houses looked like. We lived in them every day and we knew what they were like. How could I tell my elder that he did not think the Inuit have intelligence? He had nothing to say; his visit lasted only a couple of hours. He should have been shocked by the conditions in which the Inuit had to live, with no running water, no flush toilets, no refrigerators and some with no electricity.

When one goes north, one cannot miss these wonderful houses put up by the department. They are most colourful — blue, red, brown and some even orange. One would think the Inuit had a choice of colour, which they did not. The material for housing arrives by ship, already painted, in the communities of the North. There are no questions asked about where the Inuit would like to have their permanent homes erected. The department does all the choosing. When an Inuk puts up a tent or an igloo, he does not put it where it will be the most colourful. He has to think about the wind and be very careful which way his door will face. He examines the ground to ensure that the tent won't sink. I have been in these colourful houses which were put up without consideration of the weather. My family has lived in them. In the winter, during snowstorms, the doors were piled up with snow which enters through cracks in the door, and the door gets stuck, iced in from condensation which forms all around the walls. In the mornings, before the stove was turned up high and before bodies could warm up the rooms, one could skate in the corners of the rooms. By mid-day it began to thaw and water was all over the house. Some communities put up with this anywhere from three to eight months of the year. It is too bad that the heads of the department do not visit the northern settlements at these times. I wonder if it would make any difference if they did visit during the harder times of the year. What would the department heads do? Go back to sit and write about their visit, of course, to say how wonderful it was, how interesting. It is a bigger wonder why the department does not choose for the Inuk in the South where to live. There the head has a greater right to do so, knowing the South with its conveniences, and all the countless laws.

The Situation was Familiar

One day I was asked to go over to another building to meet an important man. When I arrived, there was a photographer and this so-called important man. On the table was a carving shaped like an Inuk woman, and beside the carving were savings bonds. The important man shook my hand and asked me how I was. He did not wait for my answer as he seemed rather excited over something. He directed me to a desk and positioned me there; behind me was a map of the Northwest Territories. The man directed me to hold the bonds and look at the carving and to have a big smile. Instantly the photographer took the picture.

When I went home, I told my qallunaaq about my picture being taken. She asked me right away, "Does that mean your picture is going to be in the paper again?" I did not know; I was not informed why my picture was taken, least of all for whom. She decided to get a newspaper. We began to turn the pages. Sure enough, there I was, big as life, holding savings bonds against my chest and looking at the carving with a big smile. The story read: "Eskimos buying bonds, keeping up with progress," some remark like that. I felt sick. I had no idea what bonds were. My parents had never even heard about them, let alone buy them. Today my father still has no idea what bonds are, though he has been working with Northern Affairs for the last thirteen years. I felt sick because I was being used to show the qallunaat in the South how well the Inuit are treated in the North. I recognized the whole set-up because I had grown up with the great politicians of my people and had known, seen and experienced their way of handling the community. I do not know what my picture was doing in the paper, posing with bonds. But I began to learn that qallunaat too had politics and I knew well to keep away from it when I looked at my picture. I became very apprehensive after that when someone phoned, asking to interview me. I felt I could not be a part of something which was not really happening. Never were there photographs that showed the truth about my people's lives.

II
Inullivunga:
Born to Inuk Ways

The Story of My People

It was in the early 1890s that my grandfather began his travels along the coast of Hudson Bay and James Bay, ending finally at Charlton Island. His starting point had been the Belcher Islands, which at one time he had named Weetaltuk Islands, after himself. During his stay on Charlton Island he met Robert J. Flaherty, who made the film "Nanook of the North." Flaherty had travelled from Moosonee, Ontario, looking for mineral deposits. In the course of their conversation Weetaltuk told him of an island with iron-rich rocks, so Flaherty took along Weetaltuk with his family and another family, that of my other grandfather, Symma, the father of my father. In the year 1913, Weetaltuk navigated the boat, the *Laddie*, bringing Flaherty to the islands. He then travelled back to Cape Hope Island and settled there. Again he named the island Weetaltuk, after himself.

Here he established his family. The three eldest sons had been married when they left the Belchers; there were three other sons and three daughters, two of whom he took with him and one he left at Great Whale River. One of the daughters taken with him was my mother. He travelled all the way down the coast of Hudson Bay and James Bay. At Cape Jones, they met up with Symma's family. In 1935 my mother and father entered into a trial marriage. The partnership was tested, observed and finally approved of by the parents of those on trial. In 1937 I was born, their eldest daughter. The tradition was that an only son would stay with his parents, so my mother moved in automatically with my father's parents. The families continued to travel as a group.

During this time grandfather Weetaltuk sent a note to Great Whale River, by the ship that passed Cape Hope, to have two particular women and a man brought back; he knew these people and had chosen them to be the wives for two of his sons and a husband for his last single daughter.

On Cape Hope Island he was the leader of the people, his sons and daughters and in-laws. He chose where the seasons would be spent. He performed the church services, did baptisms and burials, and divided the animals that were killed. When freeze-up came he was the first one to test the ice to see if it was safe to travel. His supply of qallunaat goods — sugar, tea and flour — was always plentiful. It was his habit to bring out these goods while waiting for freeze-up, when everybody else had run out from the last trading at the end of August, and when there would be no trading again until early December. His house was the centre of every activity: dances, church and feasting. He lacked no equipment of any sort, whether Inuk man's tools or qallunaat tools. All his furniture was handmade by himself. On Cape Hope he built a sawmill and a steamer to curve wood for boats and canoes. To this day his youngest son Pili builds boats at Great Whale River. Today there are still two boats running which he and his sons and in-laws built; one is owned by the Roman Catholic mission and the other was bought from the RCMP by the co-op in Cape Dorset, NWT. I was in Coral Harbour, Southampton Island, NWT, when this boat was being transferred from Rankin Inlet to Cape Dorset in 1971. All the memories of Cape Hope Island surrounded that boat in my visions, and my heart felt warm to think that I should see it again, a boat that was built right in front of the house where I was born. It outlived its builder; grandfather Weetaltuk died in 1957 at the age of ninety-eight. He is buried on Cape Hope Island.

After his death, the group became disorganized and drifted apart. One could tell there was no more strength left among them. They could no longer fight the intruders who were so anxious to relocate them; reluctantly, they moved to Great Whale River where many promises of jobs and better housing were made. When I visited them at Great Whale not one Cape Hope Islander had a job, and as they had not been allowed to bring their canoes

they had nothing with which to survive these strange surroundings. My father had never been idle in his life and there he was
with nothing to do. He was not willing to take handouts from the
welfare people, so he sat at home feeling quite helpless. While I
was there I went to see the administrator from Northern Affairs
and told him about my father and what he was used to doing, that
he had always navigated boats in the summer and managed stores
and built houses and repaired watches. I don't think he believed
me, as my father is one of those people who do not show their
capabilities. He is withdrawn, shy and does not waste many
words. The administrator gave him a job as a janitor at the school.
Every able-bodied person from James Bay was set back by this
move. They were taken advantage of when their leader died.

The Inuk Way that I Was Born Into

Though I can now take much for granted in the *qallunaat* world, I
still see many things, experience many moments that I will never
really understand. Maybe that is because I was not brought up to
live with its rules. My culture has rules too, but I learned them
when my bones and brain were soft, so they were easily embed-
ded and put there to stay. I keep telling myself that I have been
born twice, once to grow and learn my own culture, and again to
learn *qallunaat* culture. Once I was asked which way of life I
preferred. I said that I did not really know, and that it would take
years to explain my choices and preferences. They both have good
and bad, wonderful and sad, easy and hard times.

But it is nice to remember my own ways. My mother was
dowered to my father on the day she was born, which is one of our
rules. For this each called the other *angilissiak*, waiting-for-you-
to-grow-up. No well-classed Inuk woman can marry a poor-
classed man. But a high-classed man can marry a low-classed
woman, for the poor-classed woman is believed to make the best
wife, because she will surely need and serve him well. He in turn
has good reason to pamper and spoil her without really spoiling
her character. It is the well-classed woman who would be spoiled

in this way and therefore have a greater chance of taking over the man's manhood — he would end up the laughing stock of the community. But this kind of thing happened very seldom, perhaps when a young man had made his own choice for a wife, for it is Inuit tradition that parents choose wives and husbands for their children. Both my father and mother followed this tradition. I was born to them when they were both seventeen. In our society a young man will have learned his duties as a man, though he has just begun to learn how to bring up children. His own parents and in-laws are there to guide him, which is the case for the new mother also.

Before I was born, my mother had to decide who would be involved at my birth. During her pregnancy, many people came to ask for her consent to attend. Customarily, such decisions are based on a number of considerations. People who have asked for consent have to be considered by close relatives and immediate in-laws. Those who are believed to have wisdom of life, who are successful economically and socially, are usually favoured. The first person who has to be there is a mid-wife, man or woman. In my case it was my grandmother. While I was being born, she had to study how I came into the world. According to her, I moved all over, which she took to mean that I would be in strange lands one day. Also present at my birth was the person I was named after, my other grandmother. This automatically meant that I would never call her "grandmother," nor would she call me "grand-child"; instead, we called each other *sauniq*, namesake, bone-to-bone relation. This brought my parents and I that much closer to her. I was their security against in-law problems.

Then someone had to dress me in my very first clothing. It can be a man or a woman. Since I was a girl, the person who dressed me has to call me *arnaliak*, bringing-you-up-to-be-woman. This person, for the rest of his life and mine, has the heaviest responsi-bility. Just how I turn out to be as an adult is his job. He guided me in acquiring knowledge of the ways of people and taught me how to know myself. He lectured me on how to approach different kinds of people. He was responsible for shaping my mind. As long as I remained a child, he brought me presents on special occasions such as his hunting successes, or on the first and last trading trips to the Hudson's Bay store in the fall and spring. In return I called him *sanariarruk*, he-forms-me-into.

The most serious part of my birth involved another child. By an arrangement between my parents and his parents, we too called each other *angilissiak*, waiting-for-you-to-grow-up. That is how the Inuit child is born, and with all these people to guide me I began to grow.

I Remember

I was barely four years old in 1941. My father and mother had gone camping with another couple, and I had been left behind with my grandparents. When my father did not return from the summer camp near Cape Hope, it began to cause worry in our settlement. Two of my uncles and their families had not returned either from Old Factory. They had gone to summer there, waiting for the return of their school children from Fort George Mission School.

Taking me with them, my grandparents decided to search for my father and his party where they had said they would camp. It was a terrible trip by canoe for both grandfather and grandmother. The paddling was strenuous through the newly-formed sea ice. Grandfather was paddling and poking the ice while grandmother steered at the rear. After hours and hours, we finally sighted the camp. As we came nearer, we saw nobody. No one met us as our canoe docked, yet we were very noisy. No doubt misfortune had overtaken my father and mother; it is traditional that arrivals are not greeted when something serious has happened. I felt by the actions of my grandparents that there was something wrong.

I walked beside them across the stony beach area, up towards two tents at the edge of the trees. I was out of breath, trying to keep up with grandmother who was holding my hand. My four-year-old legs were trying their best to avoid falling, my eiderdown outfit felt heavy and I was so hot. There was a strong smell of skunk as we came near to the tent entrance. We entered. The whole atmosphere was sad. There lay my mother, looking very thin and barely audible when she spoke. She gave me love sounds that mothers made and told me not to come near. My baby brother was sitting beside her, looking very lost. Father was sitting down near her. He reached for me and gave me a long caress with his nose.

The couple that were with them had also had a misfortune. There was a lot of snow on the branches of the nearby trees. Apparently their only son had been throwing rocks up into the trees to bring down these chunks of snow. They were hard and a lot had fallen down on him, injuring one of his eyes.

We did not wait another day before my grandfather decided to travel to Old Factory where there was medical help. Three canoes made the treacherous trip, including a dog that had been sprayed by a skunk. I think every Inuit and Indian, and even the odd qallunaaq came down to see us on our arrival. The priest was notified. With all this happening, my brother and I were taken to our aunt's tent and fed with warm food while our grandparents pitched their tent. I must have slept for some time because I next remember great daylight. It was a beautiful sunny day, but everyone was moving rather sadly. I was not even reminded to go out and look at the world, just fed and dressed. It seemed that every person that came to our tent shook my hand and gave me a hug with gestures of sadness. To my mind there was certainly something missing and I knew what it was. Usually there is a lot of news exchanged and gift-giving; people make verbal relations with each other, bind it stronger; children, like me and my brother, are told how much we have grown, how smart we are with our chores. But people did not seem to be in that mood. I learned later that it was this day that my mother died. I do not know if anyone tried to explain her death to me and I do not think that I would have really understood. I did not miss her at that age, but today I often think that I would have liked to have known her.

It Was a Strange Winter

After mother's death our time at the post seemed so long and yet it was only early fall. My father and my immediate family dressed in black clothing, the symbol of mourning, for one year. It was at this time that my father began to encourage me to learn the Cree Indian language. I already knew a few sentences — come here, let's play, I am afraid, you are terrible — but to my father that was not enough. He repeatedly told me to learn to speak it fluently. He would point out some Indian children playing nearby and ask me to join them. For some reason it seemed important to him that I should learn the Cree language quickly, instead of the way Inuit have done over the years, slowly and through frequent contact with the James Bay Indians.

None of the Indians seemed to have learned our language except the word *kamiit*, seal skin boots, which they needed desperately. They would swarm around the Inuit tents in the fall, ordering a pair from every available woman who could sew them before they went to their inland camps.

When fall arrived and winter was showing its way, we did not move to our usual wintering site on Cape Hope Island. Every Inuit had gone except my family. It seemed that my father had to work for the Hudson's Bay in the coming winter. It meant that we moved to the other island in Old Factory River, right amongst the Indians. Not that they were many during the winter, as most of them go inland to catch beaver and don't return until summer. The importance of learning the Cree language became clear: I was now having to play with Indian children.

I remember only sad and strange things about that year. Our tents were pitched near the Hudson's Bay store. There were two tents facing each other in order to make extra living space for my father and his belongings. On the other side were my brother and me, grandfather and grandmother. Apart from us on the island that winter were the Hudson's Bay store manager, a *qallunaaq*, his Indian assistant Thomas Mark and his family, the Anglican missionary and his Indian wife. On the other side of the river were the

Catholic missionary and a brother, and a retarded Indian man who managed the Frère stores, his sister and her family.

Nothing seemed meaningful and nothing familiar. Even our routine had no purpose. Everyday father would go out and return only for meals and at bedtime. Grandfather did the same. My brother and I had nothing to do except help grandmother get pails of water and cut wood; while she cut wood, brother and I would place them neatly near the doorway. She did not allow us to go any further than the water hole on the river ice. She allowed us to visit the assistant manager's family only when she went. Even the weather seemed very cold and dark.

Then, the sun began to stay longer, and every now and then my father would burn something and discard items. Grandmother would explain that he was slowly coming out of his mourning. He was burning and discarding things that had belonged to my mother. One Sunday morning I watched him pick up a gramophone record and place his hands around it and crack it ever so gently in half. He put it in our wood stove and watched it melt while his face grimaced with deep sorrow. The record was my mother's favourite reel. He looked up and saw me watching him. His face changed to the loving, ugly face I knew and he gave me love sounds full of sympathy. According to our tradition he was not supposed to practise any more sorrow over the death of his wife but to accept it and let her rest. Surely if he kept his sorrow going he would go mad — that was the belief in my culture about people who had lost loved ones through death. He knew the tradition, but it seemed that he had to do it one last time; afterwards, I never saw him practise sorrow again. That summer one of my aunts had a baby girl who was named Malla, after my mother. My brother and I had to call her "our Malla," though the ending of the name was changed with *apik* which means smaller or not the real one. My mother was then believed to be resting in peace.

Finally, one day, my brother and I were sliding around our tent when we noticed a movement in the distance, at the mouth of the river. There was not just one, but a whole trail of them. I yelled towards our tent to make sure grandmother heard me: *Allaaluit!*

Indians! They were coming back. My whole inside was bubbling with excitement while grandmother stayed calm. I was not excited by the Indians, but by what would follow them — Inuit friends and relations. There would be so many to play with in my own language.

I Will Never Know Another Summer like That

Before I knew it, the whole island was covered with tepees and white tents, and the smell of branches was in the air. There were constant visitors, shaking of hands, comments being made about how we had managed so well without our mother. Then, when the month of June arrived, the Inuit came. It was so good to see familiar faces. Our tent was packed with relatives and again, comments were made and bonds were strengthened. My family moved back to the other side of Old Factory River with the Inuit. To me, the whole summer seemed all sunshine after such a long, lonely winter. I was able to visit with whomever I wanted and do my duties without feeling that I was trespassing on somebody else's land.

Most of the Cape Hope Islanders were now at Old Factory except grandfather Weetaltuk and his youngest son. Usually they never moved during summer except to come to the post and trade. Men began to put fish nets into the water, to hunt geese and ducks. Women began to arrange themselves to begin berry picking and to see who would get a canoe from her husband. Some days we would leave early in the morning and return early in the evening, at least before the men came back, otherwise no one would be home to pluck the geese and ducks or scale the fish. Arriving back was always so hectic, especially for me and my brother. We had to put everything away, bring the grub box back to its place, store the oars in a safe corner, carry to our tent the wood that we had gathered while we were out, get pails of water, pull the canoe up where it was secure and turn it upside down so it would stay dry inside. Of course, my brother and I did not do this in a peaceful way. We spent most of our time quarrelling, comparing who did the most and who did not. By the time we were finished one of us would go home crying. Neither of us would get sympathy. If one is sympathized with, one will grow up with a mixed-up nature, aggressive and demanding attention. That kind will surely end up with no respect at all from the community. So if one of us cried at home, it was a waste of tears. But one would forget to cry on approaching the tent of a successful hunter. Before one gets to the door of the tent, one smells a goose or duck cooking, and one enters and women are in the process of serving the meal, goose boiled with dumplings with lots of gravy, and fish and blueberry salad. I will never know another summer like that.

Trading was a Chore but a Necessity

The Hudson's Bay Company supply ships arrived, along with other ships that belonged to the missionaries. This event used to cause a lot of excitement among the whole community. Everybody was curious — what has arrived, what is new among the goods? The most popular item was fabric, and the women seemed to race for it. Grandmother would make a big discussion, whether she should get some for me when she got her fabric. Did I need a new dress? Did my brother need new pants? And always both of us would have our new clothes and both of us were expected to look after them and wear them only for Sunday best.

Then the Catholic mission boat arrived, and everyone would want to see the bishop, even the strongly professed Protestants. The whole dock area would swarm with people. Bishop Belleau was the most fascinating man to visit James Bay. There was something about this man that attracted both Inuit and Indians. He ignored no one. As soon as he stepped out of the canoe he would be in the crowd, shaking hands and taking time to show his ring to those who asked to see, and greeting people by their names. His attitude was most unusual and very kindly. He was not like other big *qallunaat* who came to count how many of us were left, nor was he like the ones who seemed to be afraid to be too near us, as if we were full of some incurable disease. (I'm sure most of us carried such disease, but then it originally came from them.) When the bishop gave the church service the whole community would attend, even the Indians from the other side of the river. He would cause the biggest conversation among people for weeks after he had departed.

The Catholic supply boat arrived soon after, the one that always brought sadness to me and my brother. For this was the boat that picked up our father, as he was the only man who knew the way to Fort George, where the water was deep and where it was shallow. He would be gone for one or two weeks and sometimes passed us altogether and went on to Moosonee. He would be there until the school children were ready to leave, then on to Fort George and home again. He would be home only until the boat had to go back to Moosonee to anchor for the year. Without him I always felt so lost and daily tasks seemed meaningless. When he finally returned for good, he always had presents for me and my brother, always something useful. Before he had had a chance to do his summer hunting, the season would be gone and we would have to get ready to move to another camp for the fall, usually to a spot where my grandfather thought there would be plenty of game to sustain us before winter set in.

The Indians would slowly disappear inland, and the Inuit too would leave during the first week of September before the sea iced. While waiting for freeze-up, people took time to get acquainted again and to catch up with what individuals had been doing during the summer. Women began to sew winter clothing for their families. Games were played in different homes, and children were noticed for their behaviour, growth and talents. This always seemed an indolent time for the men; they repaired sleds, harnesses, whips and all the other winter gear, the summer gear having been put away in safety. By the end of November everybody, including children, would be walking around in new winter clothes: parkas, *kamiit*, mitts, and I, as always, in my new eider-down pants.

At this time the men decided who was to go to the trading post at Old Factory. There had to be at least two teams of dogs, enough to bring back supplies for the people who placed orders. The day before trading travel, grandfather Weetaltuk would do his annual testing. This ritual has always been memorable for me. I can still see him walking out of his door, all dressed in a new outfit and harpoon in hand, to test the safety of the ice. Feeling with the harpoon, stepping where he poked, he walked slowly and did not look back. Finally he would stride boldly, without making himself lighter like one trying not to wake up a baby. Then everyone could see that he was now walking with his normal walk, slowly becoming smaller and smaller until he had no shape, but looked like a moving dot. Then he became bigger and bigger and more recognizable, until he again entered his house. In no time the news would be out that the ice was *sikuttuk*, solid ice. There would be no doubt that the traders for the community would leave the next day. This was the one night of the year that the whole community would go to bed early.

My sleepy head would hear, "Minnie, you are the only one who will miss the *qallunaaliattut*," the departure of traders for the post, those who are going to where the *qallunaat* are. This was grandmother's way of getting me up fast. On this morning I forgot that the wood stove was not yet lit; this morning I ignored the cold, crispy air in the tent and left my cosy eider-down sleeping place to watch the dogs being harnessed. The morning was so cold that footsteps made a grinding sound on the snow. One could not really see the people who were moving around, only their shapes were recognizable as the sun was not up yet.

When every item for the trip has been tied up on the sled and each man has sat himself in his place, the *pituk*, the string that holds the sled anchored to the ground, is loosened, and away the teams go. At first the dogs run tirelessly. After a while their tongues hang out and they trot at their normal pace. The man sits, his breath making smoke, concentrating on the dogs and the horizon around him, getting up now and then to take a few steps to keep warm and encouraging his dogs with command words that he has taught them to understand: *errah* for left, *auk auk* for right, *uit uit* to go, *how how* for come here, *aha aha* for even pace, *auu auu* to stop. This kind of trip is made with a grub box, sleeping bag, harpoon and gun for each man. With seventeen to twenty dogs and so little on the sled, the travellers should reach the trading post towards evening provided there are no problems, such as dogs becoming tangled too often, or bad weather.

In the meantime there was anxiety at home for their return, as some families had run out of tea, sugar, flour, coffee or oats. Borrowing a bit here and there had started sometime ago in the middle of November. This was also the time our grandmother would remind my brother and me how different things were from the days of father's childhood, when he would come home from woodcutting and ptarmigan-hunting with tea and sugar that he had stowed away to surprise his mother at this time of the year. Everyone seemed to be restless, especially children, and we would be sent off to *nasik*, to look to the horizon for the traders. This time also was the earliest bedtime for the whole community, for if the traders did not arrive tonight they would certainly be here late tomorrow afternoon. There I would be, trying to wait up for them, but constantly being reminded by grandmother: "Minnie, you are the only one who will miss the arrival of the traders tomorrow because I will not spend time trying to wake you." Who wanted to miss the arrival of the traders? Not me, and into bed I went. "Minnie, undress or you will walk in your sleep." I am sure grandmother had eyes in the back of her head.

The next morning there would be no way to keep me in bed. This was one morning that I did not count my stockings as grandmother called it. Usually it was an effort to put my stockings over my toe, over my instep, over my heel, halfway up my leg and finally over my knees. The time that I spent dressing seemed so long to my grandmother that some days she would wake me by saying, "stocking counting time." The whole process seemed to be an ordeal because I would rather sleep. But not this morning; this morning I did not even drink my hot gravy and out I went to *nasik*, to look to the horizon in search of traders.

Finally some child would come running home, out of breath, calling at the top of his lungs: *Qimmussiit, qimmussiit!* Dog teams, dog teams! An adult had to go and look to make sure. She would return and announce: *Ajjiliqut*, they are coming. Children would start running towards the traders and get a ride up to the camp. Such an exciting sight to see the dogs, now running faster having scented camp. One would hear the commands to the dogs and finally *auu auu*, stop. Nothing would be unpacked until each man had all his gear put away and his travel clothing tended. His parka had to be hung and the snow and frost brushed off the fur. His mitts would be turned inside out and hung to dry. His boots were also turned inside out and all his socks changed to dry pairs from damp ones. He had to have hot tea and a meal if he needed one. There was I, struggling at the side of grandmother, trying to turn one mitt inside out and grandmother complaining how slow I was: "Minnie, your future husband will not get very far, you are so *parqpaaluk*, slow with clumsiness." All I could think about was what we would get from the trading post. Finally, when all this was done, everyone was relaxed and all the goods were put into order, what belonged to whom. All night there would be exchanges back and forth, from house to house, as some of the items got mixed up along the way, and there would be children like me, bringing gifts to our builder, our *sanariarruk*. Trading was a chore, but also a necessity.

They Came Bearing Gifts

There was no more travelling that winter except for the men who went hunting. We stayed on Cape Hope Island all spring and summer and followed our normal spring season activities. But we had very unusual visitors that summer. A small Peterhead boat arrived with passengers I had never seen before. I had never seen *qallunaaq* other than missionaries and Hudson's Bay traders, and I did not regard the missionaries as *qallunaat*, for the ones we knew had Inuk names. Besides, they spoke my language and had black hair. I can still see myself running like mad towards our house when I noticed that these men had blond hair. I went inside and headed straight to the little window, pulled over a box to climb on and watched these two *qallunaat*.

There were two barrels near the house where my grandmother

kept her seal oil, oil which we used for *qullik*, seal oil lamps. One of the men reached down into a barrel and picked up some fat tissue and sniffed it. I started to giggle because he put it down so quickly that I could see the oil splashing up on his face. Just as I was getting down from the box, grandmother came in. She had been visiting, probably trying to find out who these people were. She understood what I had been doing. "How embarrassing! How dare you peep like that!" I tried to tell her what I saw. *Suva?* What? Splashed by oil! That episode always stuck in my mind, for I discovered two things. One, grandmother had a great sense of embarrassment over little things that I thought were normal and funny. Two, there existed strange blond people.

The two *qallunaat* stayed with grandfather Weetaltuk for some time. I know it was a few days because I was not allowed to go in and out of his house. No child was ever allowed to run around when there were strange visitors who were thought to be special, as it was considered distracting to important visitors.

After the two *qallunaat* left for Moosonee, grandfather Weetaltuk began to bring out old army clothes, old pieces of broken chandeliers and thread-snapped Victorian beads. He shared them with each household. Even I got one bead from grandmother to look at and admire. I would hold it in my little hands, examine it, turn it, and look through its hole. To me, it was so pretty. It had a white background and different-coloured spots all over it, and it was shaped like a tear drop. I kept it in my sewing box which grandfather Symma had made for me out of dried grass. Inside was a needle on a cushion grandmother had made for me out of *qallunaartak*, *qallunaat* material, fabric; it was decorated with the syllabics of my name. There was also a thimble which my *sanariarruk* had given me from one of his fox pelt trades at the Hudson's Bay Company store. The rest of my treasures were little rocks that I had picked up along the shore of our settlement, and which I thought were pretty.

Grandmother used to hate these stones; to her, they were just extra weight. To make me get rid of them she used to tell me that I was making the rocks laugh. And when I made the rocks laugh, it meant that I created evil around me, that the rocks enjoyed my creation and made evil laughs. So I used to get rid of them real fast. But somehow I always forgot about their evil laughs and started collecting all over again. Each year I grew bigger and a little stronger, and the rocks that I collected grew bigger too. I would come home from rock hunts, weighted down with rocks that I carried in the front of my dress. I would puff, barely able to walk, and drop all the rocks in front of our house. Grandmother would hear them drop and yell out, "*Ainnali*, not again!" I would puff and puff and try to put them out of the way as best as I could. In the evenings, when she was straightening our sleeping platform, she would find one or two long, black rocks which I had pretended were my dolls. Her final word was, "*Tusanngituaaluvutit*, you are definitely hard of hearing." I would get scared, not because I was hard of hearing, but because the sound of her voice told me that evil laughs would soon be heard.

At that age too, I was terribly anxious to copy the older women. Most of them were carrying babies. I began to carry a pillow. Grandmother did not like me playing with the pillows because it made extra work for her when the pillow burst or tore and the eider-down scattered all over. She would warn me that the pillow would tickle me to death. It was a belief that a person who laughed for a long time could die — *aattuq* — catch a breath and stop breathing. This is believed to happen when a person is tickled endlessly. That, of course, scared me, so I did not carry the pillow on my back.

That summer, some of the men walked around in army pants and coats and some in army hats. Most men did not go for them, and their wives used the clothes to wipe their feet on before coming into the house. I did not like them either because the men looked overpowering and strange. The smell of the clothing reminded me of the odor of the Hudson's Bay Company warehouses, and I did not like that smell. It was not the end of the strange people who came bearing gifts.

The War in the Qallunaat World Rubbed on Us

There came news that there was a big war in the *qallunaat* world, that the fighting was so great that many people were being killed. Grandfather Symma would tell grandmother of the news after we had gone to bed. I would lay awake listening, though I did not know what to make of it all. Sometimes I thought that grandfather was just telling a story, as he did to brother and me. Grandfather would go on: *Jamaniaaluit*, Germans, wanted the whole world, that was why they were having a war. I could never picture the world as round as it is on the maps; I could only picture the enormous area on Cape Hope and wonder why the Germans would want the whole world. It would be gone out of my mind the next morning, all erased by the coming day's chores.

Ships passed and some stopped. The news was still the same, that there was a war in the *qallunaat* world. One man distributed guns among the men. They were told to use these guns on *qallunaat* who wore clothing with the swastika sign on it. A picture of a swastika was drawn; this is how we would recognize the *Jamaniaaluit*. The guns had arrows mounted on the barrels and the bullets were big and pointed. I watched the men examining them; they could not get over the size of the guns. One of them commented, "Shoot a seal with this, there would be no skin left on it." Everyone put the guns away where they could not be seen, and we all lived in fear for a long time. I saw the guns only when the men cleaned them; they felt responsible for their care because they belonged to the *qallunaat*.

We began to hear airplanes, especially at night. When they were heard everybody would extinguish their lights. Some days we could see them far off on the horizon. When planes were heard, some would say, "*Alalungai*, just listen, this is the one that's going to hit us." Everybody would freeze at the thought of it. Then one summer the men were told that a man named Hitler might come our way, that we should notify the post if ever he was seen, that he too wore the swastika sign. We were mystified as we were not told why we should look out for him; all we were told was to report any man with a swastika sign. People called him

hiallak, habitual cryer, as the name sounded like the word cry —
Hitler, *hiallak*.

I began to think that grandfather Symma was not just telling
stories. Men no longer went out alone and the women were not
allowed to go berry picking on their own. Symma would tell us,
"This is what *Henriaaluk*, Big Henry, used to talk about, that the
qallunaat will have wars, that the future will be worse, that one
day our land will be full of *qallunaat*, that no one will know the
other, that there will be unrest among the Inuit." Grandmother
would ask him, "How would that be possible?" He would go on,
"Maybe not in our time, maybe in Minnie's and Miki's time and
maybe in their children's time." Whoever he was, the late Big
Henry had not been lying. Nobody ever talked about him, just
about what he had said. I know he was not an Inuk because Henry
is not an Inuk name; in fact, people who have the name Henry in
my community are descendants of this Henry. All I could tell was
that he was very respected, that people called him our dear
Henriaaluk. Today, I keep thinking about those predictions.
There may be no war in Inuit land, but I begin to see that there is
unrest among the Inuit. Certainly *qallunaat* are becoming many
in our land and the Inuit are losing touch with each other.

Did They Really Pamper Their Eyebrows?

Grandfather Weetaltuk would receive more army clothes, more
chandelier pieces, more beads and carpenter's tools which he
could not get from the Hudson's Bay Company. There was a hand
saw, file, screwdrivers and lots of nails. Later, I found out that he
used to make furniture for the *qallunaaq*. No doubt he received
these gifts from and made furniture for *qallunaaq* whom he had
known from way back, before I was born. As long as I could
remember, his house had had glass in the windows, which he
must have received from a *qallunaaq* friend. That was probably
how it began, how the *qallunaat* came to rub their materialistic
nature on the simple Inuit of Hudson Bay who had previously
depended on nature alone.

I said at the beginning that *qallunaat* means "people who pamper their eyebrows." It was never explained to me by any of my ancestors why the *qallunaat* were named that. I know for sure that it does not mean white man — there is no meaning in it at all pertaining to colour or white or man. I know for sure, too, that it was the *qallunaat* who named themselves white men, to distinguish themselves from other colours, for it is they who have always been aware of different racial colours. Inuit are aware of different races, but not of colour. I have never known or been taught to identify another race by skin colour.

Qallunaat; I have turned the word inside out to try and find the meaning. First of all the word *qallu* can mean eyebrow; by adding an ending one has *qallu-naaq*, one; two *qallunaaq* is *qallunaat* — many *qallunaaq*. The word implies humans who pamper or fuss with nature, of materialistic habit. Avaricious people. *Qallu* is also the beginning of the word *qallunartak*, material or fabric or anything that is manufactured or store-bought. It can also mean a rag made of material or fabric, or any material other than a material from nature.

Somehow I cannot see how the Inuit would have been impressed if the *qallunaat* pampered their eyebrows. I cannot imagine the *qallunaat* pampering their eyebrows when they did not care how they looked in the middle of the Arctic; even today, they do not seem to care how they look. They are so busy making money, they don't seem to have time to pamper themselves, let alone their eyebrows. Furthermore, when I see pictures of the first *qallunaat* who came to the Arctic, they always look so dishevelled in overalls, plaid shirts and heavy-looking sweaters, their faces covered with beard and their hair uncombed. For those reasons, I do not understand why the *qallunaat* would be called people who pamper their eyebrows. I believe it is the other meaning that is significant — *qallunaaraaluit*, very respectable, avaricious, materialistic, who could do anything with material, or those who fear for their ability to manufacture material. All those meanings are in that one word: *qallu*, material or fabric (man-made); *naa*, avaricious, who is proud to show his material, who lures with material; *raa*, respectable, fearing, magical; *luit*, many, human. (*Luit* can also mean they or them rather than us.) I was born too late to witness the naming of the first *qallunaat* arrivals to the Arctic; possibly they pampered their eyebrows, more likely they were *qallunaaraaluit*. Over time the word has been shortened and the literal meaning changed.

The Inuit, too, gave themselves an identity. To me the word "Eskimo" means nothing. It is an Indian word — *escheemau* — that the *qallunaat* tried to say at one time. It is a Cree word: *Escee*, sickening, can't stand it; *mau*, human. At first encounter Cree Indians were sickened by the sight of the Inuit eating raw meat. Today, the Inuit still eat raw meat and it's still *yam yam* as far as I am concerned. When we lived in Old Factory amongst Indians, we had to be very careful that we did not eat raw meat in front of them, not because we were ashamed but because we did not want to upset` them. The Inuit differentiated themselves from the animals of nature, not from other races. *Inuk* means one human; *Inuuk* means two humans; *Inuit* means many humans. *Inuk* can also mean alive as opposed to dead. Today, of course, the Inuk identifies himself as *Inuk*, different from any other race he has encountered since the days when just he and the animals of his land lived in the north.

It Was a Time of Joy and a Time to Learn

We wintered on Cape Hope Island and the men hunted, but during the middle of winter we moved to Charlton Island. One day Grandfather Symma went off on foot, looking for seals. He had walked quite a distance when he discovered some trapped whales, apparently very many. As he was on foot he managed to kill one whale and brought back some *mattak*, whale skin, a delicacy for us and normally one of the luxuries of summer. Everyone was excited about the whales. Our tent was packed while the men came to discuss the trapped whales with grandfather. The next day, there was not one man left at our camp.

During the day, one of my aunts decided to move her tent a little bit further away from the trail, as everytime the dog teams arrived her entrance was sniffed by excited dogs. To do this, she stripped the tent from its original foundation, removing the chimney from her woodstove. The stove remained, still burning. She planned to keep it going while she pitched her tent, so that the tent would not take long to warm up once she put it back in. Suddenly, there were heard the sounds of dogs barking. This startled everyone as it was too early for the whale hunters to have returned. Every head was out of the tent. One could see the dogs, all excited, and a man rolling a child who seemed to be on fire in the snow. It was my father who had just arrived from Old Factory all by himself. Just as he came upon our camp he had seen this little two-year-old cousin of mine on fire and had rushed to save her. The little girl was burned all around her chin, right up to her forehead and all her beautiful, long braided hair was gone.

The mother tended to her, and my brother, grandmother and I helped my father undo his sled. Grandmother told him of the news about the whales. We sat in the tent and joined father in a meal. I remember that part, so cosy. It was so good to see father. Frère stores had let him go to hunt. He had left Old Factory that morning, stopping a few minutes at Cape Hope and then come on to Charlton. Our tent was warm with the wood stove crackling and our bright lamp burning. Sitting with my father was rare for us. It seemed he had worked so hard for the Hudson's Bay Company and Frère Stores and on the ships since our mother had died. It was also rare for father to talk and ask questions as he was usually very quiet.

The whalers must have arrived very late because when I woke, my grandfather was talking to my father, exchanging news of the post and Cape Hope Island. Outside some of the women were tending the whale meat, sinew and skins. There was so much whale that no one bothered to divide it up for each household. Everyone just helped themselves from the pile outside.

Before long, every woman had whale skins hanging up to dry in the sun; from these she would make soles for the kamiit. The skin turns white while drying and whiter still after it has been chewed. There was no shortage of the material and even little girls like me were given skins already cut out so that we might learn how to make boots. Of course, it had to be a little pair. I decided to make a pair for my brother, but grandmother pointed out that I had to give them to my *sanariarruk*. Like all children, I cried because I wanted my brother to keep what I made. But customs are customs, and when I finished I had to walk down to my *sanariarruk's* tent and give him the boots. He hugged me and gave me all the praise that I wished for. It encouraged me, so I went home and asked to make another pair for him. But no, it had to be something else. It was only the things I made for the first time that went to him, such was the promise that had been made when he had dressed me when I was born. My grandmother then said that I could make a pair for my brother. Like the first pair, I chewed the skin to soften it, and grandmother made me patterns for the sole, instep, heel and the leg pieces. After cutting the sole into proper shape, I then had to cut the instep and the heel into shape and fold them in half so that the edges were even, and then put them in a container to soak for awhile. This part is tedious as one has to be careful the skin does not soak too much, otherwise it will go right back to its raw stage and become hard to handle.

I sat near the container, asking grandmother every few minutes, *namasivaat*, are they ready? Finally I took them out, handled one and put the rest under a canvas so they would not dry out. While I was waiting for them to soak I made ready the sinew to use as a thread and found a good needle. It cannot be any old needle. The length and the shape of the eye has to be just right so that it will not be hard to pull through or cause the skin to split. The thread is tested by running it between the teeth and feeling it with one's tongue to find any broken or weak parts. The strand has to be the shape of a carrot; the narrow end is purposely shaped so that the very small eye of the needle can take it, making the tiniest, waterproof, strong stitch around the edge of the skin. The sole has to be pleated so that it comes over the instep part and is shaped like a moccasin slipper. Having sewn the instep and heel together, one has to go right around to put the sole on. When that is done, it has to be turned inside out and reinforced by sewing in the instep piece. Then one sews big stitches with a knot on every stitch to secure and shape the heel. Again, it is turned right side out and softened by rolling it between the hands and stretching it with special stretching equipment made of wood and shaped like the boot. Then the boot is left in the air to dry properly. While waiting for it to dry, the leg piece is cut, shaped and sewn. One has to be careful with this part. The legs are made of seal skin fur. For boys and men the fur has to run downwards. It can be decorated by sewing different colours down the front. The fur for girls and women runs sideways and can be decorated sideways. (The direction of the fur is just a convention similar to the practise of qallunaat men and women who button their shirts from different sides.)

At this point, the women usually take a break or do something else while waiting for the feet to dry, or they make strings for the legs which are threaded in and out through little holes that are about an inch apart all around the top part of the leg. Each end of the string is crossed over the other; when you pull them, the whole top part of the leg pleats and prevents snow from getting in. The foot parts are then sewn on to the leg parts. Finally the boots are finished. The experienced women can make a pair in a day, but it took me three days to finish a pair that fit a four-year-old. All the little girls of my age were making boots, there was so much material around. It was indeed a joy and a time to learn for our future so that we might take care of our husbands and children.

To Learn is Sometimes Painful

Indians came to our camp and were welcomed happily. The purpose of their coming was to trade goods or money for boots, mainly spring boots which are even more tedious to make than fur ones. One man wanted three pairs and planned to stay to wait for them. Every woman and girl was chewing skins for the next couple of days. There was grandmother chewing and reminding me endlessly how to do it properly: "Minnie, do not chew without interest, think about partridge berries and your mouth will wet more and you will finish chewing that much faster. Hold it this way and go back and forth, turn it on the other side every so often. If you chew without attention you will only tire your jaws." I had to learn so many things that year, probably things I would have to know for the sake of my future. I had to give up many things that I preferred doing, such as going into the woods with my brother, hunting ptarmigan, putting up snares for rabbits, gathering spruce gum and looking for the tracks of the foxes, and carrying babies on my back for the other women. To learn is sometimes painful, not being able to do what one wants.

It was Peaceful

By the beginning of April, the men were talking about moving to a good goose hunting area. Grandfather decided that the whole camp should move because we had to move anyway to get back to Cape Hope Island before the ice became too thin on the sea. At that time Charlton Island was the best goose hunting area known by the James Bay people.

After spending time on the south side of the island, we moved to the northeast; there it is hilly with rock, and there are partridge berry patches where the geese come to feed and nestle and get fat. It was here that my brother shot his first goose, an event which excited me very much. My brother and I may not have gotten along peacefully, but whatever he did for the first time was always so lifting for me. Excitement always made me forget about traditions and customs. Whatever he killed for the first time always went to his *sanariarruk*. That surely brought my enthusiasm right down to the ground. It would take me a couple of days to get over my disappointment at not being able to enjoy my brother's hunting success.

It was a beautiful month; the sun was shining, beating down, doing its job to melt the snow and thin the ice on the sea. Men never seemed to sleep now, they just watched the geese. My father would sit for hours at the point, not far from camp, dressed in dull-coloured clothing so he would not be spotted by the birds. My brother and I would take turns bringing him tea during the day. By the time he came home, we would be asleep. Waking up the next morning, the aroma of fresh goose cooking would hit my nose. I would pop up my head to see who was up, and there was my grandmother, already plucking more geese.

Whether she was sitting with her back to me or sideways, she would know that I was awake. "Minnie, you will bear unhealthy children if you stay in bed any longer. Go out and look at the world." My imagination would go to work and I would picture my unhealthy children. But I could never picture a baby of my own; always it would be people I knew with some kind of handicap. My uncle, who was crippled, would flash through my mind; one of our dogs who had one small eye; an Indian man who walked with twitching movements. (It is only today that I understand what my grandmother meant by "unhealthy": those who are spoiled, lazy or unkind, liars, stealers, cheaters and hypocrites.) How could I form those kinds of children just by staying in bed a few more minutes? I had to get up and look at the world around me; it was peaceful.

No More Baby Hammocks

The goose hunt never lasted long — the thinning of the ice always forced us to move before it became too dangerous to travel. But before we left the area, the men had to hunt seals, which by this time were basking on the ice. One morning my father decided to take my brother and me.

We left the camp with nothing on the sled but the three of us and a grub box, and the dogs just shot out after their long wait for freedom. My brother and I sat behind our father, hearing every command he made to the dogs. It was all such a new experience. This was the first time we had ridden on the sled without being put in the uqugusik, the hammock-shaped baby place. It made me realize that we were regarded as babies no longer. It was different and much more strict for us, not being able to move or talk loudly. In the uqugusik we were always able to play and talk and move anyway we wanted; our voices did not disturb the working dogs as we were muffled by canvas and blankets. I found it strenuous just sitting on the sled, not able to fool around, but it was something else that my brother and I had to get used to.

Finally our father turned around for a minute and asked us to scan the horizon for the seals. This was also a new skill to be learned. Then I saw something dark quite far away, and poked my father on the back and pointed to what I saw. He looked and then turned back at me and said with a very loving voice: "Old woman," which meant it was no seal at all but a dirty piece of protruding ice. How silly I felt! Suddenly father stopped the dogs and directed my brother to keep the dogs quiet with the whip. He set off to stalk a seal, slowly, stopping now and then until the seal put his head down. Now I felt very tense. I wanted to watch my father but my brother and I had the job of keeping the dogs quiet. Not all of them were willing to rest; a couple were alert and kept making anxiety noises. My brother said, "Be ready to jump on the sled; when the dogs hear the shot they will not wait for you." I pictured myself being left behind and never catching up. That made my body even more tense. My brother seemed so relaxed. I stood near him and wondered, is he not afraid? Will he be able to handle the dogs? This is also his first trip out, maybe it was natural for him, after all he will grow up to be a hunter.

It took ten or fifteen minutes for father to come within shooting range of the seal he was stalking. Bang! The dogs sprang up all at once and it was one mad scramble — some dogs were too fast for the others, some were caught on the legs by traces and one was so doped with sleep that he was dragged and his trace slipped under the sled. I was puffing and trying not to drag my feet when we reached my father and the dead seal. There the scramble began all over again, the dogs were so excited and began straining for a taste of the seal's blood. Father cracked the whip over their heads and quieted them. He said that there were two seals at this hole by the looks of the area where they were basking. He more or less talked to himself, as he probably felt that we were not adult enough to hear such news.

When the dogs were settled, he motioned my brother toward the seal breathing hole. I could hear him saying, "The seal will soon come up for air and this one you will harpoon." My heart jumped. How cruel of my father to burden my little brother with such a responsibility! I watched him demonstrate how to hold the harpoon; instantly, I imagined my brother being pulled down by the seal through the hole, never to be seen again. I began to whimper and tears came down my cheeks. I had been very warm from all the excitement but I began to get cold. I could hear father, "before his nose appears over the water, aim." Splashing sounds could be heard and there was my brother, holding on with all his strength. I pictured a very big seal, but when he began to pull after some struggle, out came a little seal. The very first seal of my little brother. "Nassiputit," announced my father. "You have got your first seal." It hit me then that my brother had begun to be a hunter; he was carrying on the old traditions and ways of survival that had sustained my people for centuries.

Father said that we would have tea, also our first. Our grandmother had not allowed it, believing that it was strictly an adult affair to have tea. We had our tea, which I liked only because of its sugar content. Father looked at the little seal and said to my brother, "You again have something to bring to your sanariarruk." What could I say to that? When we got back I did not bother to help unharness the dogs, I did not even pick up anything to take to safety. I just got off the sled and went straight to our tent. In the tent there was no one, they were all down at our sled. I cried and cried. I would never see the seal again — it went straight to my brother's sanariarruk, skin and all.

I stopped crying when everybody came, but acted so isolated that I finally caused an argument between my father and grandmother. Father said: "You know the rules; when are you going to teach her that there should be no ugguanik, no sorrow seeing something go, through stinginess. It is time to start now, or we will have problems, and she will suffer when one day she has to leave us." He was not angry or blaming grandmother, only enforcing our rules on how to bring up children. In fact, he was talking to me indirectly; surely I would change because I did not enjoy the unpleasant argument between the two people I needed most. Inuit parents have long used this technique to straighten children; it is the best weapon and it saves constant scolding which children can begin to take as a challenge. It worked on me. I had to accept our rules and traditions. After that, pleasing others was a pleasure. My brother and I were out of the baby travelling hammocks, but I would rather stay home and tend the seal skins than endure that kind of educational travelling.

The Doll Lasted Much Longer on the Wall

The thinning ice finally forced us to move back to Cape Hope Island. There we waited for the ice to break up. And, of course, the trading season came. Only parents who had children in school went and stayed in Old Factory; there they waited for their children's return. Summer passed, and some children went back to school and the parents returned to Cape Hope to wait for the freeze-up. Winter arrived again, but this year there were different plans for the men. Three teams of dogs went to Moosonee to trade.

It was very exciting to the whole community, as Moosonee was considered to be the source of everything. I was told that I would get a doll, a real one, not made of rags or stones. I was given the doll, but I never got to play with it; my grandmother's idiosyncracies would not allow it. She kept the doll hanging on the wall, right above our *qullik*, our seal oil lamp. To her, it was too beautiful to play with, so she treasured it. I was allowed only to look at it. I used to climb on the table, trying not to knock off the *qullik*, to feel the doll, but I was always caught by grandmother. She never really scolded and only told me that I will have it that much longer. I used to think that since I am going to have it that much longer, then I should play with it and she can hang it when I have had it for a long time. To me, the wall had it and I did not. But still, the way I took it was that the wall would give it much longer life and I was not going to.

Nature can be Mean

After trading at Moosonee life went on, but the men were visiting each other more than usual, discussing something quite serious. I felt in my bones that something was happening. The women were sewing much more than usual; our old tent was repaired even though it had already been put away for the winter. I was made a new pair of eider-down pants. There was something happening.

The following winter three teams of dogs left Cape Hope Island, travelling towards Moosonee. Grandfathers Weetaltuk and Symma lead two teams and my youngest uncle, with his wife and new baby, lead the third. The rest of the Cape Hope Islanders, five families, were left behind. Between Cape Hope and Charlton Island a terrible blizzard came up and we had to stop. We could not see anything, not even the other people with us unless they were very close. Even then, they were a haze, but we knew by their shapes and by their manner of movement who they were. We stopped and tried to make camp, but everything was blowing away, our tents could not stand up. Finally, after the men had fought strong winds and blowing snow, all three sleds were put upside down to hold the edges of one tent. In this one little tent were six adults, two children and one baby. The dogs were not even taken from their harnesses, just left out there all curled up with one another. Though different teams of dogs will fight between themselves, they, too, seemed to understand that they needed each other to survive this terrible storm.

Giant Berries

The next day was just like *pinguartuk*, like fantasy. The sun was out, and nothing moved, not even the snow. Everything was frozen crisp. The dogs were all covered with a hard snow crust and when they tried to shake it off, some of the lumps stayed on their fur. Some began to realize the change in the weather and growled at each other, awaking to the differences of the teams. But they were all eager to move. In front of us was Charlton Island. It was so big and so close and yet we had not been able to see it the previous evening. We passed an old cabin which stood up amongst the trees. Grandmother said, "You used to live there when you were a baby." She did not actually say it like that; instead she remarked that my little foot marks were up there near the cabin.

We made many stops for tea, for relieving ourselves and to rest the dogs. Finally, we arrived at Moosonee, right in front of the Hudson's Bay store. I had been asleep in the *uqugusik* and woke to hear my grandfather making sounds for the dogs to be still, *auu auu auu*. I popped my head out of the blankets and faced grandmother who stood before me with an apple and an orange in her cold hands. "*Paungaaluit*," she said, "giant berries." I tasted apples and oranges for the first time. I ate so many that I had a terrible tummy ache for two days. They were indeed giant berries and they gave me giant pain!

Grandmother Sometimes Needed Help

We put up two tents right near the dockyard. On top of my tummy ache, I had a terrible cut on my forehead, the result of my own clumsiness with an axe while trying to help cut tent poles. I did everything with my cut, scratched it, played with it, and examined it, until it developed into impetigo which covered my whole face. The word *naniasiutik* began to be mentioned often by my grandparents. It can mean medicine, nurse, doctor or a person who tends the sick. To me, it meant horror, fear and pain.

Grandmother made two attempts to take me to this horrible place. Each time I ran right back home, taking long detours through bushes, along the beach and up the bank to our tents. Grandmother was usually successful in making my brother and me obey her wishes; it was only when it became impossible that she called on our grandfather to do something with us. On this occasion she had to. Grandfather just took a sheet off our bed and folded it into a triangle. He stood me on the sheet, wrapped it around me and turned his back, then crossed the ends of the sheet around his chest and away we went to the hospital. Nothing was said. I could not utter a peep, I was so shocked.

Entering the hospital, I panicked. A dark figure opened the door for us — I was trapped. The figure wore a long dress, a black veil and a black hood over its head. There was also something hanging on its chest, something that looked familiar because I had seen it in the book my grandfather read to me every evening, teaching me how to read and write. The figure brought us to a long corridor, up the stairs and into a little room full of beautiful bottles. There was another of these strange creatures in the room in similar clothing, but all in white. They spoke to my grandfather with a language I was used to hearing — Cree. That was my first encounter with the Grey Nuns of the Cross. They and grandfather helped grandmother to calm me down, which she sometimes needed.

Grandparents Seemed to have Made It for Me

Though Moosonee was a strange community to me and my brother, we still got into a lot of mischief. He and I used to take off for walks along the sandy beach. Sometimes we just gathered junk that we found. Moosonee was full of garbage, the dirtiest area we had ever been to. No matter how often we were told not to bring anything home, brother and I always returned with handfuls of old beer bottles, tin cans or whatever we thought was pretty to play with. It was a constant worry to our grandmother who thought we were taking things from people's homes. That is something we dared not do, as we were too afraid to go near strangers. Sometimes we took a walk down to the dock area and sat by the bank of the river and watched Indians coming and going in their canoes. We loved to hear their strange Cree dialects; some words struck us as very funny and we would walk home, imitating their sounds.

I had not known the purpose of this move to Moosonee, but the following spring and summer of 1943 grandfathers Weetaltuk and Symma and my young uncle started to build a boat. The boat was named *Notre Dame L'Esperance* and was owned by the Roman Catholic mission. I later travelled in this boat back and forth to Fort George and Old Factory River, going in and out of Ste. Therese School, which was run by the Grey Nuns of the Cross at that time. It seemed that my grandparents had made the boat for me, and that it was meant to take me to another world.

III
Qallunanillunga:
Among the *Qallunaat*

I Was Dumped

The boat was not finished by September when the missionaries gathered all the school-aged children to their schools. I was one of them but my brother was still too young. The missionaries had already come around once to our tent. After that I would hear grandmother and grandfather discuss school and me. Grandmother was very much against it but grandfather said that I had to go. It was just like him. He always believed that refusing people in authority would lead to a bad mark on the refuser. I would hear grandfather explaining over and over that I would be home every Sunday in the afternoons and every summer. Grandmother would question him, "What is her reason for needing to learn the *qallunaat* language?" I never found out how they came to agree, but they both crossed the river from Moosonee to Moose Factory and delivered me to St. Thomas Anglican School.

The three of us were taken upstairs to a little room; sitting there was a great big man who made my grandfather sign papers. I still wonder today what the papers said. Grandmother was crying, the first time I had seen tears in her eyes since I had been in her care. I did not cry. I was too busy looking around. Without any farewell, I was taken to another room by a strange lady. She fascinated me. With her hair and red lips, she did not look at all human.

She brought me into a room with a tub of water, put me in, and washed me all over; her hands were so pale against my little brown body. All my clothing was changed and then I was lead to a huge room. There it was very noisy, but the noise was familiar to me; the room was full of Indian children. The lady silenced them with a little whistle which hung around her neck. She called the name of Elizabeth Mark. Elizabeth was the daughter of the Hudson's Bay store clerk at Old Factory River. Her parents knew mine very well, and we children knew each other.

I was just becoming used to hearing the Cree language; though I could not put words together, I understood everything that was said. Elizabeth became my translator. Everytime something was going to be done with us, Elizabeth was asked to explain it to me. As time went on, all the girls were divided into two groups: junior and senior. I was in the junior group and Elizabeth, in the senior. I saw her all the time except during class hours and at bedtime when I needed her most. I understood nothing in the *qallunaat* language, least of all reading, writing or arithmetic. Art work, I loved.

I soon adapted to the strange routines of the school. Some things I took very seriously, others I thought were just like playing house. I dreaded meal hours because I hated potatoes and turnips, and their bannock was terrible — it felt gummy in my mouth. I forced it all down because I had learned not to leave anything; if I did, I was made to stay until I finished. A few times I could not force myself. I would gather it all in my mouth and out it would come with the force of a strong leak in a canoe, all over the floor. Luckily, I sat at the end of the table. I would be put to bed, my forehead would be felt and my temperature taken. That's when I felt most lonely, in this great big bedroom with two hundred beds in it. There I began to think about my home, my food and the freedom out in the air. I never fell asleep until all the other children came to bed. With one hundred and ninety-nine Indian children I was the only Inuk child, for a total of two hundred girls. I was learning two languages at the same time, one with three different dialects.

I went home on Sunday as promised, though I saw my family only once. The next Sunday, when the principal and his crew brought me across from Moose Factory to Moosonee, my trained eyes could see that the tents were gone. I wanted to tell the crew that my relatives had left, but I could not. They all looked so huge that I did not dare say anything. We approached the dock area and landed. Finally, one of the men noticed that the tents were not there. We did not bother to climb up the bank of the shore. We turned right around and went back to the empty school. All the other children had gone home for the afternoon. My little mind told me that my grandparents had not come to say goodbye to make it easier on me. They had warned me in the past that their tents would be gone sometime soon, but it did not hit me until it happened.

My Feet were Smelly but They were Warm

By Christmas I had found my own playmates, but I still hated meal hours. My first church service was horrifying to me. Being the smallest of the juniors I was always put in the front row of seats in the chapel, as in the classroom. The preacher seemed awfully close to me, his voice so loud, and his face mad-looking. I walked out of the first service because the preacher kept shouting, "Minnie, Minnie." His glance toward me now and then and his arms waving all the time gave me the notion that he was telling me to leave. Nobody stopped me on my way out. Once I shut the door behind me, I did not know what to do. No one was around as everyone was attending the service. I went to the girls' room. I climbed onto the lockers and entered the bathroom through an open air vent. I sat on the toilet for a long time. I wondered why he had sent me out.

It seemed hours before everybody returned. I could hear the girls asking and wondering where I had gone. Why did she leave? Where is she now? Maybe she got scared? Maybe she felt sick? Poor little Inuk girl! With all that concern I began to feel a lump in my throat. Our supervisor unlocked the bathroom door, which was kept locked whenever the room was empty for some time, and she talked and asked me questions. I understood nothing of what she said, though her voice told me that she felt very bad. I started to cry with all my might. It turned out the preacher had been saying "many, many" in his sermon.

Long after Christmas, Elizabeth and I received letters from home. Hers was written in English from her father, mine was written in Cree from my grandfather. He knew Elizabeth could read for me. Along with the letter came a parcel: a pair of *kamiit*. Having been away from home for some time, the smell of the *kamiit* seemed awful to me. Some girls began to make comments and vomiting sounds, saying, "Eskimo, Eskimo." Elizabeth said, "*Kachitoo*, be quiet," and remarked that my feet would be a lot warmer than theirs.

I Think I was Kidnapped

By springtime I had learned to speak like the Cree children and had learned their Indian games as well as some *qallunaat* games like numbers hopscotch. The food was no longer strange. I loved peanut butter sandwiches the best.

All the children began to talk about going home for the summer holidays and they gave each other their names and addresses. The dates were set for each child's departure. Mine was not. It did not bother me, because I did not really understand what was going on. Nobody tried to tell me anything. I could not even remember what home was like, nor did I feel that I missed anything terribly. Finally, one day, I was completely alone. Everything seemed to be different. The supervisors, whose rules I had had to obey, suddenly began to hold me on their knees. I ate with them. They took turns taking me for walks to the Hudson's Bay store. They even had me in their living room late in the evenings. I became very attached to one of them; his name was Mr. Lake. It was the same man I would meet in Ottawa at the young people's meeting many years later. Apparently my bed was right above his bedroom, and when I could not sleep I used to cry. He would hear me and come up to read me stories and lull me to sleep. He would come up in the mornings and take me to the dining room, holding my hand. He took me for the longest walks, swung me on the highest swings, and took pictures of me wading in the mud. I thought I had been kidnapped, but they were pretty kind kidnappers.

They Came to Get Me but They Had No Ransom

Before I knew it, the school children began to come back again. Some were familiar faces, some new and strange. I never got home myself, and the new school year was beginning again. Some children asked why I did not go home, and because of their questions I began to ask the same thing. The mystery grew and grew until it reached some of the supervisors. One child was told that all my family had died. I did not understand what it meant, though I knew the word death.

The winter came with the same routine and rules. I began to understand a little more about numbers, reading and the meaning of a *qallunaat* education. Playing outdoors was always something I looked forward to. My favourite spot was near the laundry, right underneath the window, where there was a hollow in the ground that made a nice little nest for me. The window was always open and the laundry matron would peep out and tell me how cute I was.

It was one of those days when a group of girls came running, calling my name and pointing down at the gate. When I looked, I saw two men approaching. They came closer, and when they entered the gate my little heart jumped and a lump came to my throat. There they were, my grandfather and father. They had come to see me, all the way from Cape Hope Island. I am sure they had come to get me out of school and take me home as they had brought all my Inuit travel clothing. All three of us were brought to the little room where my grandfather and grandmother had left me a year and a half earlier. Then I was sent back to the girls' room and did not see them again until the following evening. I do not know what was said in that little room, but they did not come back the next day, nor the next, nor the next, until finally I put the memory of them out of my mind. I am sure they had come to take me home, but I guess they had no ransom.

So Much had Happened while I Was Away

When the summer holidays came again, I went home to Old Factory River in a little airplane. It was on a Sunday and people were just coming out of the church when we arrived. By the time I got to the shore by canoe (the plane had landed on the water), the whole beach was packed with people. There were so many and I felt so shy. Someone brought me up to the bank and there, in a little group, were all my relatives, all supposedly dead. Grandmother was crying again.

As it is an adult affair to give news about who has died and what has happened to other people, my brother began to tell me in his own way about who had died while I had been away. Two of my uncles were gone; one had died from a bladder infection — he could not shoot his bow and arrow, as he put it. The other had died of a hemorrhage of the brain. My brother said that he went mad because he had too many things to think about. As children, we were always told not to think too much, because if we did we could easily go mad. No doubt that was one way to behave and a way of forgetting, too.

We stayed the whole summer at Old Factory River. The following fall, before the school ships came around, we moved back to Cape Hope Island. I was kept home that winter. It was so wonderful. Everything came back to me, the seasonal routines, and grandfather Weetaltuk testing the ice to see if it was safe to travel.

School Is Not the Only Place of Education

That year we wintered in the cove of Cape Hope Island. The men hunted for seal, while the women and children snared rabbits and hunted ptarmigan. I think this was the year I felt closest to my grandparents and father, even though they were always away hunting. By the time they came back it would be dark. There would be so much to attend to, their gear and clothing. This was also the year that I heard many stories. One evening my brother and I and a cousin were sitting with my grandmother who was sewing a pair of boots. My father was visiting our aunt next to our tent. Grandfather was asleep. Grandmother began the story about *inuppak*, the giant.

There was a man who was very stingy. He was so stingy that he lived by himself, under his *qajak*, so that no one would know when he had returned from game hunting and he would not have to share his food. His neighbours had given up trying to get him to be kind. His answer was always, "You only want my belongings." Finally, he was warned that he would turn into a bloodthirsty giant and would belong to another kind of people who did not really exist. His usual reply was, "You only want my things." Then one day he went hunting on foot and secured his *qajaq* and his things so that no one could get at them. While he was away, something happened to him. He came back a huge man with claws that turned inwards. Perhaps this man had become a bloodthirsty giant, or the giant may have eaten the stingy man himself. The lesson is that one should not be stingy; it can be fatal not to be sharing.

Some of my ancestors were very good storytellers and the stories were passed on verbally from generation to generation as we did not have a way of writing. Everything had to be told from memory, just as we always memorized the landscapes of our hunting areas. Each generation had to carry them in their heads and tell them year in and year out. Sometimes, someone would invent a new one. Here is my contribution to this tradition, a story that I invented, but a story that is not very delightful to pass on to my children.

Nakuk was sitting on the sleeping platform, enjoying his brand new son with his wife, Maviak. He was feeling very happy, as a son is important, especially in his country, the Arctic. As he ages he will have a helper and a provider when he can no longer hunt. Hunting is his only source of livelihood, as it is to his fellow Inuit. The main game they hunt is muskox. While enjoying his son, he conversed with his wife, dreaming that his son will be a great muskox hunter one day, chattering away that he will be a great dog-team and *qajaq* traveller, that he will have the best equipment for his hunting needs, even better than Nakuk's own. Maviak sat listening to him with an admiring smile; she could not help half laughing at Nakuk. She was thinking, "My husband has already equipped our son while his navel cord is still freshly cut-off." Though she was amused by Nakuk's dreams, deep in her heart she wished the same.

But for now she wanted only to enjoy him, to cuddle and love him. She was wise enough to know that this helpless child would not be helpless very long. And if he grew as fast as Nakuk was dreaming, she would no longer be able to cuddle and love him. She finally spoke, saying, "Nakuk, what about a name for our future great hunter?" Nakuk came out of his dreams and without hesitation said, "We will call him Malittak." He had not been dreaming all the time, he had been concentrating on the muskox, which had been rare during the last two years. He began to explain to his wife why he chose the name Malittak. Malittak means "he is followed." He said that maybe the muskox would follow the birth of their son and the herds would be many again. His wife replied, "That is a big hope; it is his strength and good health we should hope for. He is only an hour old and we are already asking of him too much." "I am thinking about his strength and good health, that is why I hope the muskox will be plentiful," retorted Nakuk.

The daily tasks of Nakuk and his neighbours were endless; there was always something to be done with sleds that had broken on the last hunting trip, dog traces that snapped on sharp ice blocks, new ones to be made to replace the ones that had worn out, new harnesses to be made for the dogs, skin clothing that needed repair. Boots had to be replaced as they wore out and shrank from being soaked and dried too often. There were many chores but they had, too, the occasional entertainment amongst themselves. Nakuk could still remember the entertainment that was given for him on the day he married Maviak. Now he was thinking about a feast for his newborn son. He went about his neighbours, telling them the date of the celebration. The feast itself was very serious. It was not meant to be like the one that was usually given when an animal was taken, which was always gay with everybody excited and laughing. Nakuk planned everything for this occasion and he made it serious, more so because of his desperation that the muskox return.

He chose five persons to take part in the ceremony. Each of the five brought a symbolic gift. The feast started off with a gathering in front of these five people. The first man had three muskox stomachs; he burst each of them and scattered the contents all around the ground. This meant that the muskox will have plenty to feed on. Second was a woman who had a bundle of muskox hair. She went about and scattered the hair, meaning that the muskox will know his place. The third was a man who had piles and piles of muskox bones. He held one bone and flicked every other bone with it; this meant that many will come. The fourth man had a whole carcass of a muskox which he buried carefully, indicating that no waste should be made of the muskox carcass. The fifth man had bows and arrows made of muskox bones and tusks. He stood them in the ground with the points facing up; this meant that no hunter should kill any more than he needs, and above all never to terrorize the animal. Everyone was still.

At this moment, Nakuk happened to scan the horizon towards the sea and noticed a strange umiak, a boat. It came nearer and nearer and stopped in front of their camp. Nakuk spoke, "Do not move, I will go and see." He walked down and greeted the two men who had come ashore. The people on the hill watched and could see the three men waving their arms in all directions. After some time, Nakuk finally left the two men and came back up to his people with a very sad and disturbed expression. He returned to the spot where he had directed the ceremony and spoke: "Today I had hoped to build strength for my new son. It is not so now. The two officials from the qallunaat world have asked us not to hunt muskox for the next fifty years." He sat down, preoccupied with his private thoughts, while his people began to leave in remorse. He became aware of Maviak, carrying his new son wrapped in a baby muskox skin. That skin, he thought to himself, would be the last muskox skin he would ever handle, and so he spoke to Maviak: "We are very fortunate that our son will never have to know how to hunt muskox, for he is fresh and will have the strength to be a great seal, polar bear, whale and narwhale hunter. Yes, he is very fortunate, for this we will name him Arlu — Killerwhale — the most feared and relentless hunter of the seas."

That year, I may not have learned more about numbers and the ABC's but my learning went in other directions; school is not the only place of education.

Pain, Pain and More Pain

Spring came again. For some reason we did not go goose hunting but made a move to Old Factory before break-up. There we spent the spring and summer with our usual summer activities. Then September came, and all the school-aged children were being picked up again.

Bishop Belleau asked the parents to gather at the priest's house. My grandparents would not have anything to do with the meeting. The mission sent a messenger, asking for my father. Father went and simply told them that my brother and I had not been in his care since our mother had died. So, our grandparents were asked to come. Grandfather went alone and as he was leaving our tent, grandmother urged him to be strong. "For a change, don't let them take you over!" She knew him well, that he always gave in to what he called authority, for the sake of keeping peace and to prevent bad feelings. He was gone for hours. When he came back, he announced that I would have to go back to school. The first thing grandmother asked was, "What about Miki?" Miki means young sibling; it was the name grandmother had given my brother. Grandfather replied, "Him, too."

Grandmother had never shown any determination in matters decided on by grandfather. She followed his wishes with no complaints. Such was the tradition that my ancestors created in order to ensure successful marriages. But this time no one could change her mind; Miki was not leaving, not ever, not as long as she lived. She spoke over and over about her fears that my brother would grow to manhood while at school, that he would become a poor hunter, that he would come back (if he came back at all) spoiled, pompous and without any sense of responsibility towards his land. It was too much for her to be left by us. She devised a compromise and told grandfather (which was also against our traditions — to order a man) that they would go back together to the mission. She gave all her reasons why Miki should not go to school, and she got her way. I had never seen her so determined; it gave me fear to see her talk so much all at once. Her alternatives were that neither of us would go or just I would go, but never my brother. She has managed this; my brother never left grandmother, even though he had his own family eventually. Grandmother was still living with him, and died in his house, in January 1974, at the age of eighty-nine.

Much later, I learned that her biggest worry was that my brother and I might convert to Catholicism. Though she feared that, she decided to let me go to Fort George to Catholic school because it was much closer than Moose Factory, and besides, all my cousins were going to Fort George. But I think it also had to do with the fact that while at Moose Factory I had not returned home for two years.

So, I went to Fort George with my three cousins and an Indian girl, whom we knew very well, and her three brothers. There were four other Moosonee Indian girls already on board. We were given all night to pack, but had to be at the boat before six in the morning, the hour we were leaving. I wanted to cry so much but I was not allowed to. It was one of our traditions not to cry at departures. It is believed that crying for some one who is leaving can cause something to happen, such as a death while away; in effect, one has practised sorrow before it even happens. Of course, I feared that, and it is still in me so strongly that I always have to prepare myself before seeing a friend or relative off on a journey.

My father walked beside me down to the boat, talking all the while. "You must be obedient, you will experience no punishment that way. Never tease the other children no matter how they tease you, just go away and do not retaliate. Don't touch other people's things. Just do what you are asked to do, you will find it much more pleasant. It will not be long before you come back. Do not waste your time being lonely for home, because you will learn nothing that way. If I hear any unpleasant news about you, you will have failed me and make me live with embarrassment. And you will not become a Catholic; if you are asked, you have to write to me." How my father knew that all these things would challenge me, I do not know. His last warning was, "I do not want to see any tears when we reach the boat." I climbed aboard the boat, so did my father for a few minutes to give me a package of gum, a hug and a long nose caress. How hard it was to keep tears away at that moment.

A young priest supervised us to bed after a hot cocoa drink. Sleep did not come to me for a long time. I could hear every movement that was made, the water smacking against the boat and the French language being spoken somewhere up on the deck. Before I fell asleep, all I could think of was my little brother, my grandmother, my home, my duties and all my relatives. The last thing I felt was the motion of the boat and my stomach moving with it.

I had expected to be awakened at a certain time by our supervisor but he let us sleep until we woke ourselves. We were already moving and I was anxious to see if we were still anywhere near my home. I sat up and my stomach began to move. I felt so sick. Someone called, "She's awake," in Cree. The priest came down and asked if I would like to eat. I said yes, when I should have said no. I forced everything down. Then I was told to dress warmly and come up on the deck. I looked all around; no where could I see the settlement I had left. There was nothing but land in the distance and water ahead of us. It was a brisk, sunny day.

I sat down where the other girls were sitting. It seemed everything had changed overnight. There was nothing that looked familiar but the sea water. The crew I had never seen, the boat I had never sailed in, though it had been built by my grandfather and all my uncles. The girls I had never met before. The cousins seemed familiar, but their attitudes were strange and they spoke Cree the whole time. The eldest cousin began to encourage the rest to laugh at me by making comments: "She has decided to become good and go to our good school." That kind of treatment was most unfamiliar of all; for one thing, her parents were very strong Protestants and she had never attended the Catholic church at home unless the bishop was visiting the settlement. Then she began to tell the girls how I lived at home, how I was never free from duties, that my grandparents were old and very Eskimo. The rest of the girls began to make vomiting gestures, and she looked so smug for having succeeded in her intentions. One of the older Moosonee Indian girls was not impressed, and she told the girl to shut her mouth. My feelings were so much in pain and so lonely; I kept hearing my father's advice. I have never told him what I went through and did not wish to, because I know what his answer would have been: "Do not bring home tattle tales, it is ugly on you." That was something else I had to control many times.

During the voyage, I forced all my meals. I am one of those people who suffer seasickness. The whole trip took from 6:00 that morning to 7:00 P.M. the next day. I kept as far away as possible from the other girls during the whole trip.

Getting Used To Is Part of Survival

Arriving at Fort George was even more strange. The crew that I had begun to smile at disappeared. The nuns seemed to be so many and all looked the same. The girls I sailed with knew what to do and knew the school rules as they had been there before. All of them understood French and spoke Cree during playtime and English in class. I had a little Cree and English but no French. Then the local school children came, some young and some old, all of them Indian children. All together there were fourteen girls, ranging from six years to sixteen, five boys, from six years to fourteen, two priests, four brothers, eight nuns, two servants and one janitor.

Gradually I began to know who was who. Everything was routine, up at 7:00 A.M., wash and dress, make one's bed, and line up at the foot of the stairway by 7:30. Down we went to the second floor for morning mass in the chapel. At first mass seemed so long to me; I would get very hungry and some mornings I would faint and find myself in my bed. During breakfast there was absolute silence. Anyone caught whispering was made to stand in a corner. Each child had a chore to perform for four weeks, the task changing at the end of the month. My first chore was sweeping the stairways. Two girls worked in the dormitory, one girl helped in the kitchen, two girls worked in the dining room, one girl helped in the dispensary, one girl in the laundry, and one girl at the father-house. The rest helped in the girls' playroom. I felt a bit insulted with my chore as it was nothing to me and there was no challenge. I found it very boring, but I did not complain. Each girl had to be finished before 9:00 when we had to go to our playroom. There we washed, combed, and straightened ourselves, then lined up at the door to wait for the hand bell which our teacher would ring for class.

In the class, we said a prayer, sang *O Canada* and *God Save the King*. We memorized catechism for half an hour and one of the priests would come up and give us religion lessons. Each of us had to stand up and recite what we had memorized. Our teacher would then come back, and we would study history, spelling and arithmetic. All was silence during class unless we had to speak for our teacher. Other days we would have home economics, sewing and knitting, learning ingredients and baking. Some days we went for a stroll and some days we would have library day. History, I could never understand. The four continents or the nine (at that time) provinces of Canada did not mean anything to me. I had no idea what Canada was. As far as I was concerned, there was only Cape Hope Island, Charlton Island, Old Factory, Moose Factory and Fort George and all the little islands that I knew by their Inuit names.

Our teacher also made certain that we learned the Cree syllabics, which were very similar to Inuit syllabics in that area. She announced that an airplane would come by Christmas time and that we should write to our parents and should know our syllabics by then. That excited me and for the first time since I had come, I thought about my family. But I did not think about them long, as we were too busy. We never had idle hours except some Saturdays and Sundays or during holidays; we still had to do our chores but there was not so much routine during those times.

I do not know how we were chosen, but four of us girls took piano lessons. We had to practise everyday for an hour. I used to welcome this hour, as well as class hours, for from the time I arrived until my father came to pick me up, I was terrorized, teased, and tormented by the other girls, no doubt instigated by my eldest cousin. Not one girl was allowed to play with me while we were outside. During skating, someone would push me; at bed time, someone would hide a wet facecloth in my bed. If someone was caught talking while silence was in order, I would be blamed. Whatever chore I was responsible for would be messed up and, of course, I would be told that I did not do my job. If someone else was punished, actually caught by our supervisor, one of the girls would announce that I had told on her. I was not allowed to cry in case my tears were noticed and I was warned that I would suffer more if I went near our supervisor with teary eyes. I had no choice but to suffer in silence. I was so alone, so many lonely moments when chores and classes were slack. Christmas came and we had some holidays. It seemed so long before class hours came. I did my chores as long as I could and took my time either sweeping stairways, peeling potatoes, ironing, cleaning at the father-house or at the dispensary. In any of those places, I could be me, the girl my parents had brought me up to be, happy, enjoying chores and most of all free from fear and pain.

Bad Pains Have Good Rewards?

I have always believed that whatever bad experience a person goes through, which he does not seek or does not will himself to go through, there is always some sort of reward in some other way.

Sometime in the month of February 1946, one of the servants came down with a flu and had to be put to bed. Then one of the girls got it, one of the priests and one of the nuns. Indians began arriving at the dispensary with the flu, and soon every one of the beds was filled. Every morning, fewer of the girls could get up. The whole school was in chaos. Someone was trying to cook, someone trying to tend the sick, the laundry piled up, the school could not go on. Around the fourth day of this chaos, our supervisor came with thermometers while we were still in bed and took everyone's temperature. When she got to me, she said, "Up," and the rest were all in bed. The whole school got the flu except me. Sister Superior decided to put me in a spare room so that I wouldn't catch it. I did not believe this, as I expected to get the flu like everybody else. Everyday I felt my head when I awoke; everyday, when I went to the bathroom, I would look into my eyes and search for some sort of sign. But everyday I looked healthier and full of energy.

The nun who was the first to take to her bed was soon up and around. She looked pale and weak. I had to help her. She and I prepared the food and brought it up to the sick. I emptied all the toilet pails at outdoor outhouses. Twenty buckets in all. Each pail would turn my stomach to the point that my tongue would hang out and my breakfast hurried to my throat. By the time I got out of the outhouse I would be blinded with tears and the cold air would sting my eyes as I ran back to the school. When I reached the entrance the buckets would clang noisily while I tried to open and shut the doors. This would go on all morning until all the pails were emptied, sometimes twice a day as the sick were being given a lot of liquids.

In two or three days another nun was up and around. One evening this nun and I went down to the village to attend to the sick. On our way, I saw a man enter the father-house. I was certain that it was my father. I tried to tell the nun, but she spoke only French, very little English and no Cree, least of all Inuttitut. I kept pointing to the father-house and she just looked at me. I repeated, my father, my father, pointing to the house, even though I was a little scared in case I was mistaken. Nothing was understood. I was aware that nuns and school children were prohibited at the father-house unless it was cleaning time, so I gave up trying to tell her. As we passed by the house I raised myself on my toes to catch a glimpse of my father through the big window. I was certain that I saw my father's head. I did not say anymore.

Down we went, she with a bag of medicine and I pulling a sled, also carrying medicine. That particular evening was very cold. She would not allow me to enter the houses and tents of the villagers. I stood outside and waited for her at each home. I was so cold and began to shiver. Finally I could stand it no longer and started to walk back slowly, thinking that she would catch up with me. But I reached the school before I saw her coming. I just left the sled near the door, went in, and headed straight to the kitchen and the wood stove. I heard the kitchen door shut and knew it was the nun that I had left in the village. I panicked, thinking that she would scold me for leaving her. I did not dare go and meet her at the hall. I could hear every movement she made, dropping her bag, taking off her coat, changing her boots and shaking her long dress. She came straight to the kitchen. I must have looked petrified, for she came over and patted my back and said, "Poivre fille, avez-vous faim?" She fixed both of us a meal and put everything on a tray. She brought the tray into the girls' room and let me eat there.

While I was eating the phone rang up in the nun's living room, which was right above the girls' playroom. There was a square hole covered with grill work on the ceiling of the girls' room that allowed one to look into the room above. I could hear everything through that hole. "Oui? Son père? Oui!" Her voice sounded excited and so was I. She came down and told me that my father was coming. I could see she was not sure that I understood her. I understood every word she said. A few minutes later my father arrived. I wanted to cry with happiness, with sadness, loneliness, and over all the responsibility I was carrying alone. The lump in my throat was hard and the tears so hard to keep away. My father's teachings about crying stuck in my mind. He looked small and sheepish and seemed to say that he would break his rule for once and he urged me to have a good cry. Once he gave me that permission, however, I could not cry.

I sat near him just feeling close while he gave me love sounds that Inuit fathers make to their children. In my culture we have three levels of speech — baby speech, teenage speech and adult speech. I noticed that he was still talking to me in baby speech. He could not tell me how things were at home, that was an adult affair. He was not sure how much I knew of teenage matters, for a teenager I was under our system of growing. He did not realize how much I had been forced to grow emotionally in such a short space of time. So, he sat there telling me how much I had grown physically, and he repeated all the advice he had given me in the past. He brought me a parcel with a pair of *kamiit*, a parka and a pair of black woollen stockings from grandfather Symma. Surprisingly, I was allowed to wear them that winter. He said that he wanted to take me home but I was not allowed to leave, mainly because the priest was now responsible for me. So I stayed. My father came to visit me a couple of times more and then went back home.

Before long the epidemic passed and everything was back to its normal routine. Even my old enemy, the instigator, returned to her troublemaking, but somehow I did not care anymore that I was so alone. I found little things to do on my own. There was a statue of the Virgin Mary in the girls' play yard with a fence around it, the Grotto. There I played most of the time. I began to talk to the statue but I made sure no one could hear me.

Then spring weather came, and we began to prepare for the concerts and stage plays that we put on at the end of the year. The whole village came to see us perform. The girls let up on me because of the excitement. Everyone was wondering what she would be and what kind of costume she would wear. Opening night came. We had been resting all afternoon and in the early evening we put on our plays. I never enjoyed anything so intensely as I did the plays; the way they were put together fascinated me and the acting was a challenge. After that, everytime we had library day, I took out books on plays. That performance marked the end of the school year, but there were still a few tasks to be completed before all the school children disappeared back to their homes. We had a sale and exhibit of all the things we had made during the year. The whole school put on a sale of the clothing that had been sent from the south to this mission. The village was notified of the event. Every child was going back and forth from the warehouse to the boys' playroom where the sale was going to take place. I was going back and forth too, but alone, while most of the girls were in pairs.

I came out on my way to the warehouse, about my fifth trip. I took a short cut by climbing the high verandah, instead of using the stairs. I was just in the process of climbing when the father who was principal of the school came over. Before I got on my feet, I could see his black shoes and the long black dress hanging over them. When I looked up, he seemed cross and his face had a mask of deep pain. I realized that I had done something wrong, I was not supposed to climb the verandah. I said, "Hello, Father." He looked at me rather hesitantly, so I just kept going towards the warehouse where our supervisor was handing out the clothing for sale. Then he stopped me and spoke with a shaky voice, "Minnie, your grandfather Symma is dead! We just had a talk with the priest at Old Factory, all your parents are there now and your father is on his way to bring you back home."

I wanted to reach the priest to cry, but I controlled myself as I was afraid that he might not allow it. I stood there on the verandah and sobbed. Our supervisor walked me back to the school and comforted me. It seemed I was spared from the pain of the flu epidemic, but meant to suffer mental pain over my dear grandfather whom I had regarded as a father since he and grandmother adopted me the day my mother died.

A Mourning Trip

The parents of the local children began to claim them back. Finally, there were only ten of us, four Moosonee girls and a boy, three of us cousins and two boy cousins. Though I could not forget my torment, the instigator began to melt towards me. I felt neither compelled nor eager to acknowledge her sudden friendliness. Perhaps if she had been so earlier, I would have been delighted. I felt that I had gone through enough; nothing that happened or was said to me would hurt me again. This was the girl who I so feared at the beginning of the year, and now I no longer feared or respected her. How odd that fear and respect can go together.

My father arrived and had a message that all my cousins were expected by their parents to return home with him. The priest in charge felt responsible for our safety and therefore asked the younger priest to accompany us on our way.

It was a beautiful June month. The sun was beating down, warming the air. Hudson Bay was so calm that one felt like walking on the water, it looked like beautiful blue ice. There was not a wave stirring and all one could hear were seagulls fighting over a fish or sea-clam. We travelled in one motor canoe and another we towed contained our belongings. When the two canoes were readied we boarded and my father expertly examined the motor. With a flick of his hands and a pull on the string, the motor started and off we went.

The familiar smell of the sea got into my nostrils. My mind was happy but my heart heavy, as my father and I were in mourning. We did not stop until we had found a place to camp overnight. This I could not understand because it seemed that it was only lunch time. I knew my father would have kept going to take advantage of such a nice day, to travel as far as possible. Then I realized that there was a stranger amongst us, the priest, who was not used to travelling such long distances. My father felt responsible for him as he realized that the priest was entirely in his hands; he needed extra consideration, a practise my people have followed whenever a stranger travelled with them. The priest was not aware of the consideration he was being given, nor would my father sit down and tell him about the responsibility he felt towards him. To me, the two men looked like two priests, one guided by God because of his profession and one guarding the other because of his sense of responsibility for another human being.

After our meal the priest let us wade in the ponds and puddles. He was an avid photographer and he took movies of the trip and of us children wading. When the tents were being pitched up, the priest had more items and junk than any of us. I have always thought of him whenever I see an anthropologist getting ready to go to the Arctic. They are the worst junk carriers that I have met — junk in the sense that the items they take with them are unnecessary. Sometimes they brought items that they did not even unpack for the whole year of their stay in the North. They cause the biggest worry to their guides during travel. I know because I am married to one, though I have tamed him a bit about packing over the years.

From Fort George to Old Factory River is about one hundred and fifty miles, not counting the fiords and points one has to follow to keep a safe distance from the shore. I know that a ship can leave Fort George at six in the morning and arrive at six in the evening, provided the weather is good throughout the trip. But with a little canoe and motor, it took us about a week and a half. As we neared Old Factory River, we began to see Indian camps. We had tea at one camp where my father was known, and we were offered some sun-dried fish. How delicious the fish was! The Indians, always hospitable to my father, laid down a lot of fish in front of our tea fire. I had two fish and was ready to have another when my father said, "Minnie, think. You have not had that for a long time, don't have too much all at once." Gradual eating habits are practised in my culture; if one has not had a particular food for a long time, one does not eat too much at once as it can cause one a nauseating sickness to the stomach which we call *kavalinniq*, turned off from too much indulgence.

We proceeded on our way until finally we rounded the bend of a long point that cups the Old Factory River. Across that point every scene was familiar. I had come to recognize that view after years of arrivals at Old Factory River; I knew that I had reached my summer home. I looked at my father who was steering the motor. He smiled with that ugly, kindly, sun-tanned face, but looked so tired and heavy-laden. I was filled with excitement, but also sadness, knowing that no one would come to meet me at the beach where we docked our canoes, as is the tradition when there has been death in the family. As we approached the beach we could see all the Indians and Inuit relatives of my cousins. My brother and grandmother were the only ones missing. Once again, I could hear all around me the expressions of sympathy that I had heard so long ago when my mother died.

My father told me to go on ahead as he had to attend to the gear and see the young priest to the priest-house, thereby fulfilling his responsibilities towards him. Aunts and uncles walked along and pointed out our tent. I entered and there sat grandmother, crying, and brother looking so sad. I could not hold my own tears, so I sobbed silently. Grandmother no longer looked tall and proud as she always had; she looked tiny and lost. Even her corner of the tent was very unorganized. Certainly the head of the family was missing! She was all in black, even her seal skin boots had black trim. When she realized that I, too, was crying she spoke, "We will let him rest in peace." She stopped crying and soothed me. Then she turned on me and said, "We will see if your mind is as womanly as your body appears to be. My, you have grown into a woman!" Though I knew that she was complimenting me, somehow it did not seem important how much I had grown. All I asked in my mind was, "How are you going to do, grandma?" I knew that, like all Inuit women with a quiet and reserved nature, she had always been the backbone of our family, and in that respect she was strong. But she had lost the companion that she had come to rely on since she was fourteen years old and now she was fifty-two.

My brother sat at the other side of the sleeping platform looking grown and sad. Grandmother ordered him to go and help our father with the gear. In a while, they both came back. Father dropped all his gear, which grandmother later had to tend, near the doorway. He sat down and had his hot coffee without a word, quiet as he always had been. Only his face showed that he had sudden responsibilities ahead of him. After his coffee, he spoke to grandmother. "I know it is hard for you, but they [meaning my brother and me] are both young and we must try our best to erase the constant reminder of death among us." He was only following our tradition, sparing his children this atmosphere of sadness. If only he had known how much my mind had grown in such a short space of time, able now to understand his silent suffering; the speech I could have made for him would have broken him into pieces. I let our tradition take its own course. But it took a week for me to realize how much I missed my grandfather; things were not done that were usually done when he was around. We did not have such plentiful supplies of food and meat. Usually by this time of the year our fish nets were in the water, but they were still bundled up in a burlap bag, just the way he had put them away after mending and straightening them out, all set for the next use. It was indeed a mourning trip in every way.

Desperate Chance

It was not long after our arrival that my father became very sick, so sick that he was delirious with a high temperature. Everyone who had some kind of knowledge of medicine was asked to see him — the Catholic missionaries, the Hudson's Bay manager, the Anglican minister, the owner of the Frère stores. Father was so sick that he could not even take the shine of daylight, it pained his eyes. Our tent had to be covered with dark material and our stove constantly on fire as he was shivery and cold. It was predicted that he would not live.

One of the constant visitors was the wife of the Frère store owner; no doubt, she felt she owed much to my father, as he was the one who took her to Fort George when she needed transportation and when she could not wait for the ships. He had worked for her family for so long that her three sons treated him as one of the family. She came in to see my father almost everyday and looked desperate what to do. Then one day her visits gave me an idea. I knew that she lacked no spices and I was certain that she would have mustard. My only problem was to work up the courage to ask her without feeling shy. But by this time, seeing my father suffer so much was agony to me. I asked her if she had any mustard and she said yes. I began to tell her about the health and emergency lessons we had had in school; one of the medications we had been taught was a mustard plaster for pneumonia. A feeling in my bones told me that that was what my father had.

She was very eager and suggested that we go to her house to fix it, that I would have to show her how. We went up the little hill towards her house, the only *qallunaaq* house other than the missionary's, all the rest being tepees and canvas tents. I had been in her house only by invitation from her daughter and had never been any further than the porch, which was the custom for Inuit children who were visiting. We entered her house and I stopped at the porch while she took off her shoes. She then invited me into her kitchen where she laid out mustard, flour, utensils and thin cotton.

We went back to my father and warmed the plaster on our stove. We spread it where my father had the pain, right on his side above his left hip. Again, because of our custom that a child is not supposed to express knowledge towards elders, I waited for the woman to ask me how long it should be left on. I told her and explained what could happen if it were left too long. She came everyday and asked if I needed any more mustard.

A couple of days later, my father began to be aware of his surroundings and his temperature became normal, though he could not sit up because of dizziness and weakness. He asked for food and drank lots of coffee as was his habit. During one of the woman's usual visits, she asked my father if he was pleased that I had gone to school. He did not comment, but just gave the twinkle-eyed, kindly smile that is his well-known expression of gratitude. He began to sit up and our tent-hold gradually returned to normal. For a while, grandmother would call my father in the middle of the night saying, *"Irningai? Irningai?* Dear son, dear son."* She had been doing it for the last three weeks to check if he was alright. My father answered, *"Ee, ee,* yes, yes."* Hearing him answer without a pained voice let me know that I had done right, taking a desperate chance in using the mustard plaster on him.

We Almost Had an Indian Mother

It was very hot that summer, so hot that the black flies and mosquitoes never let up until late at night. Everyone had mosquito nets inside their tents, so one might sleep without being pestered. One of my aunts urged father to sit outside everyday and went out of her way to get the kind of food he craved.

One afternoon I watched him sitting in the sun. He looked so thin. I wondered why he had never married again when mother had been dead for all of ten years. Several trips had been made and letters exchanged with Fort George to find him a wife as there was no one eligible in our community. One particular woman named Nellie was a high choice of grandmother's. I heard so much about her, how sweet and kind she was, but that she did not want to leave her home. Her parents had already consented, but she did not want to leave. People said that she had even packed her belongings to leave, but always changed her mind. I never knew what to think about the whole thing. At my young age I did not see anything wrong, that my father had been a single man for all these years, until I began to hear people worry about it. Then I learned that it was not our way to have a capable man live alone for so long.

One day we had a visit from an old Indian couple. They came to ask my grandmother if my father would like to marry their daughter. My father's answer was, "I would not know how to hunt beaver." They assured him that he would be taught wisely how to hunt beaver. My father gave a polite chuckle to let them know that he did not mean to insult them, and told them that they had a beautiful daughter but that he could not think of leaving his way of life. The Indian couple were very traditional beaver-hunting people and my father had no doubt that he would have been taught well how to handle Indian hunting skills. But that was not the only obstacle; just as the Inuit culture has many beliefs and systems, my father knew that so do Indians. He was not about to begin a new way of life at his age.

My brother and I began to tease each other about having an Indian mother. "*Naja*, sister is going to have an Indian mother," and I would retaliate that he was the one who was going to have an Indian mother. Neither of us considered that whoever married our father would be mother to both of us. As long as we had something to say to each other that was a little mean or ugly, that was all that mattered in our minds. How childish we were!

The summer got hotter and hotter while my father became stronger and stronger. His ugly, kind face tanned so brown, almost black. He began to take short walks, and the first place he went was to see his motor and canoe down at the beach. No doubt he was anxious to travel again. He had never been idle for that length of time. He did not navigate the boat for the mission that summer, which made my grandmother glad, mainly because she felt that he was not that strong. All summer she kept worrying about him and constantly reminded him to wear a warm sweater other than his black mourning sweater for the death of his father. That summer passed by with our usual tasks, scaling fish, picking berries and finally plucking geese. Then it was time again to move.

We wintered on Charlton Island where my grandfather Symma was buried. Grandmother and I visited his grave a couple of times. Again we hunted goose the coming spring. My brother was my father's constant companion. I could see father aging very fast; he probably felt the heavy responsibility that was his. My brother and I got to know him better than we ever had; for one thing, he spoke to us a lot more, either to order us, lecture us or to tease us with loving gestures.

Father Knew How to Hold Our Tongues

The whole camp began to move back to Cape Hope. It was a beautiful sunny day when we hitched everything on the sled and set off. The middle of the bay was quite safe, but as we neared Cape Hope the ice became thin and there were potholes all around the coast of the island. We were about half a mile away from our cabins when I decided to walk along with our team. We had been warned not to step off our sled as it was very dangerous because of the thin ice. Everybody knew the rule, the different ways of travelling at different seasons, including my brother and me. We were being treated as growing children and were trusted to obey the rules, so we were no longer put into the uqugusijavvik.

I figured that my father would not know if I took two or three steps — I would be back on the sled before he knew it, or at least that's what I thought. Down I went! It was very strange that the dogs suddenly stopped themselves. Father turned around and there I was, up to my armpits in the water, holding on to the edge of the sled. I was getting cold fast. My eider-down pants were soaked and the only dry spot on me was my parka hood. Grand-mother was yelling, "Get her before she goes down!" No one stepped on the ice. Father crawled along the sled to get to the rear in order to reach me. I looked back at the hole as father pulled me out. It was dark and cold looking! Our sled had to be undone so tediously, without getting off, in order to get a blanket to wrap me in.

Here my father had trusted me to stay on the sled during the whole trip. My brother and I had been taught to endure discomforts on long trips during dangerous travelling seasons, such as springtime. We had been warned in order to prepare ourselves, since it was our first experience travelling on an open sled without the *uqugusijavvik*. But it seemed I had to learn some other way, and that was the last time I stepped off the sled during spring travel. There was nothing else that could be done but go on. The land that was nearest to us was all rock and high cliffs straight down to the sea. There was no way father could try to take our sled over those rocky hills.

I had seen father when he was a little irritated, when I did not listen to him right away. Now he was so mad that words were not coming from him. He turned to my brother and said, "I will leave you if you step off the sled!" That was his last warning and we arrived at Cape Hope without words, too stunned to take even a deep breath. No one else had arrived. There was no place I could go to warm up. Grandmother took off all my clothes and wrapped me in dryer blankets. I could see my father was still very mad by the way he was working, unlashing the sled and bringing our gear and belongings to the site where we would put up our tent. All kinds of feelings were going through me: fear, rejection, guilt, and frustration at not being able to do anything. To cover these feelings, I scanned the horizon now and then, looking for the other teams, so I could announce when I saw them and make it known that I was being useful and helpful. But my inexperienced peepers could not tell dog teams from dirty blocks of ice. I wanted so much to see the other teams first, but I think my father had already known they were coming when I finally spotted them. It was just not my day!

Our tent was up and our stove put in, usually a man's job, by my father. The inside of the tent and settling-in was the job of women, which grandmother was doing. I was supposed to be in there learning and helping, but there I was all wrapped up in a blanket, feeling quite helpless. The fire in the wood stove was soon roaring, and grandmother came out to take me inside the tent. She already had all my spare dry clothes ready to put on. The smell of tea, gravy and coffee was in the air. The bannock was thawing near the stove. In a while, we all sat and had hot tea, coffee and gravy with bannock. I looked at my father who was sitting on his own side of the tent. He became aware that I was looking at him. I must have looked rather sad, because in his eyes was a twinkle full of love that lit up his face. Forgetting and forgiveness were in the air, and my brother and I slowly let loose with our tongues.

How Grandmother Got Flat Fingers

The rest of the camp arrived, and every woman and child came in to warm up and have tea. The biggest news was that Minnie had fallen through the ice, thanks to her disobedience. Should I speak for myself? Scream? Laugh? Show humiliation? No, I must control myself, that is the custom, so I sat there taking it all.

It was a wonderful, idle time again as it was spring. This was the time when everybody became re-acquainted, while the ice was in the process of break-up. Again, people were lending and borrowing from each other the store-bought items that were getting low. The sun began to stay longer and made everybody look brown and burned, while glistening snow caused snow blindness to those who were careless with their eyes. Preparations were made to move to the trading post, to Old Factory, as usual. On our route, we stopped at a little island to pick goose and gulls eggs and to make tea. Everyone enjoyed the tea, even more so because of the eggs. I never cared much for goose and gulls eggs; somehow I connected their taste to rabbit meat and I never liked rabbit meat.

Finally we arrived at the narrows of Old Factory River; from there we could see the red roofs of the Hudson's Bay store, the church steeple and many tepees and white tents. When we reached the beach, the Indians were all down to welcome us. Though we did not know them all that well, they were familiar from the many visits we had made over the years. My parents had known them much longer, as their parents had been around there since the late 1800s. They knew who was related to whom, and who married, and who had a newborn child, and who it was named after. Whenever there was an Indian wedding, the Inuit were invited to help celebrate, and they in turn did the same. Every Indian had an Inuit name, not because the Inuit have a habit of name-calling, but to identify the individuals among themselves. No doubt we, too, were given individual names by the Indians. My father was called Thomas Symma, only the Indians pronounced it Simone as they could not say Inuit words. They meant that my father was a son of Symma. And I was called Thomas Symma *utanish*, Thomas Simone's daughter. I had a cousin who was called *Pichogee*, Gum Crazy; he was always chewing gum.

Though Inuit and Indian adults got along and respected each other, and small children did not see any difference, teenagers always picked on each other. If an adult was not around to correct them, they tried to imitate each other's language. But I have never known of any serious discrimination between the Inuit and Indians. They needed each other for celebrating weddings and feasts. Indians needed seal skin boots every fall before they went to their inland camps.

As the years progressed, grandmother made boots for regular customers, and as the years went by, she knew the Indians that appreciated her work and paid her well. She knew the ones that kept saying, "When the beaver man [Indian agent from the South] comes I will pay you." Every summer the beaver man would come, but no pay for grandmother. As the years went by, she made boots only for the well-paying individuals. The ones that appreciated her always made a special trip across the river to pay her. Others would wait until Sundays; when we crossed the river to attend the Sunday church services, they would make an effort to meet her after and pay her. But the ones that did not pay simply ignored her, and she knew when the avoiding was being done on purpose, and she would simply say, "He will need boots next year and will have to face me then." So some were forced to pay that way, but grandmother never went to demand her pay. I knew a family that owed her money for over five years. When grandfather died, the family came to express their condolences and paid her in full. She tried to discourage them since it was so long ago, but the Indian family would not have it that way.

Grandmother took the money and bought a whole outfit for her *arnaliak*, the child she was building. She bought a pair of high rubber boots for my father, summer jackets for brother and me, some yardage of canvas to make a tent for father's hunting needs. The only thing she bought for herself was a package of gum, and then she ended up sharing it out. When I think of it today, it does not seem fair, especially when she earned the money. Until the day she died, her index finger and her thumb were slightly flat from pulling the needle and sinew thread so many times in her past, and her teeth were worn down flat from chewing the skins to soften them.

Common to Natives, But Not to Doctors

We settled again for the summer. School children arrived. Berry picking and fishing began. Boats brought the yearly distinguished visitors.

My brother and I were very attached to our father, at least he seemed to want us around more, now that he had the chance. Every month during summer he would take us to the Hudson's Bay Company store to spend the family allowance. He bought us an outfit or socks or rubber boots. He never bought us anything that was sweet, or if he did, he would hang on to it and give us one candy a month. He was not a stingy man, but to him too much candy was too much of a luxury for his children. If we had a lot of gum and candy, it was usually grandmother who splurged for us.

Once we accompanied father on one of his trips, and we

started out early in the morning. Father said that he was going to try and beat the crowds to the store. It did not necessarily mean that there were a lot of crowds in a big line-up, like the supermarkets in the South. In those days, people in small communities knew everybody and everything that went on, and when they got together at the Hudson's Bay store, they discussed matters in their own time, and never minded who was waiting to be served. That's what my father meant by beating the crowds – it was to beat them before they got too involved in discussions.

Father had some special friends among the Indian men. If he met them before he met the store clerk, he could end up playing checkers with them for hours. It happened that very day we were with him. My brother and I were too shy to stand around and watch along with the others, so we played hide and seek at the beach near one of the Hudson's Bay Company warehouses. It was fun to have such freedom from chores, until it got later and later, and we became hungry. Finally he came, only to check that we were alright and to give us some dried fish to eat, no doubt from one of his Indian friends. He said that we could go and visit some Indians we knew, but not to stay long. We did not, as we were too shy. As the afternoon progressed, it became windy. The checkers players began to pass by on their way home, and father came at last. The three of us went down to our canoe, boarded and headed back home across the river. I looked at father in the rear of the canoe. His face, which looked so old, was concentrating on our route, trying to avoid the rocks now that the tide was out.

That same evening, all I wanted to do was to play with my doll, and I did something that I had never done before – I was the last one in bed. Grandmother kept urging me to go to bed, but she eventually fell asleep until I dropped something and woke her. "Are you having the last time of your life?" she asked, for that is a belief when someone stays up late without reason, especially if it is to play. Father had been visiting our aunt's tent and he came home late. He looked very surprised when he saw me still up. I should have been very tired, especially since I had been out in the air all that day, but I felt wide awake and finally forced myself to bed.

The next morning I felt nauseated, but could not vomit. My whole body felt weak. I did not tell anyone how I felt, because I knew I would be put to bed. It was a beautiful sunny day, the sun beaming down on our white tent. I could hear grandmother outside near the door, scraping seal skin with a steel scraper. I could smell the fresh shavings of the skin that my brother and I usually ate. We ate them like qallunaat eat potato chips, only their taste is like that of unsalted bacon. Somehow she knew that I was awake. "Minnie, come out and look at the world." There I sat, counting my stockings as grandmother called it, over my toe, my ankle, my leg and my knee. I found it an effort to dress. Grandmother came in and noticed how listless I was, and even father asked if I was sick. I said no. I sat on the wooden box near our stove, which was still going after breakfast had been cooked. I sat on the box thinking that I should move around so it would not be noticed that I was ill. I got up to join grandmother with the oats she had made for me. Just as I picked up a spoon, my hand felt hot and full of needles pricking me. The pain climbed up my arm and when it reached my neck I became dizzy and must have fallen as I do not remember anything else.

When I came to, all my relatives were crying around my bed. One of my aunts was putting a wet cloth over my forehead, pressing and rubbing. The sun was no longer shining in, but our whole tent was covered with extra canvas so that the sun would not hurt my eyes and as a sign to the community that there was a sick person in that tent. The missionary priest had been called and apparently he gave me a shot of needle.

I have tried to explain this attack several times to different doctors, but they do not know what it is – either they don't know or would not tell me. But the Inuit call it qisurtuk. I cannot translate it in one word, but it is an attack that can occur anytime and it is believed that most people who get it grow out of it. Old people believe that it is caused by heavy responsibilities which weigh on a young mind, a mind that cannot yet cope in an organized fashion. My aunt knew how to treat it because she had a son who used to have it when very young. Sometimes it strikes girls and women who become chilled just before their menstrual cycle. It is also believed that anyone who does not grow out of it gradually grows smaller in size. As the attack occurs, one uses all one's inner strength to fight it, and having used one's inner strength, one grows smaller. There was an Indian woman who had these attacks and who never outgrew them. Indians call this *ocheepitoko*, the pulling sensation. Sometimes this woman had it once a year, sometimes twice and sometimes she would miss a couple of years. She gradually grew smaller and looked weak and not very alert. Everyone noticed with sympathy, knowing what she goes through everytime she has an attack. She stood out, as Indian women tend to be tall and lank before they have middle-age spread.

My aunt began to say that I had passed the worst stage of it, but that I would be weak for some time and that maybe one of my legs and feet would look like it was pulling upwards, which it did. This grows out too if it is treated the way it should be, the patient made to walk with it until it comes back to normal. The double tent-canvas that had been thrown over our tent was lifted, but I still had to stay in bed. I had two more attacks in later years, but trust that I have now outgrown it; the last was twenty-four years ago.

She Had Cold Hands, But the Least Painful

Again the first ship arrived and the usual excitement went on. I had no idea that I would have to leave on that first ship to go to Fort George. My father had been told by the missionary that I should have a proper medical checkup. That very evening my father carried me on his back to board me on the ship. At that moment a heavy loneliness swept through my body. It seemed I could never stay long enough on this familiar ground, on the land that was so much a part of me. There was always something to make me leave. I wanted to speak to the ears of my father, who was carrying me on his back, and tell him that I did not feel sick, that I was well enough to stay home. Then again, I thought that he had to listen to the authorities who seemed so much more knowledge-able.

We reached my father's canoe, and he got the motor going, and off we went to the ship that was anchored half a mile away. I looked to the horizon; it was calm and there were many seagulls flying around. We passed our berry-picking place and I hoped that I might be back when they were ripe, that I might help pick them with the women. We reached the ship and father slowed his canoe. Father helped me up on the deck and one of the crew showed him the cabin I was to occupy. He took me down to it, and there again I received the lecture that I had heard so often at my departures. Father went back up on the deck, but I did not follow him because I knew I would have tears. The sound of his motor faded away. We left within a few minutes. I lay down and began to feel the motion of the ship. My stomach went with the motion and I felt sick all the way. I decided that the only way to forget my misery was to go to sleep, but sleep would not come, and I lay there reliving my departing scene. It seemed I had done this so often that I should be used to it, but each departure was harder than the last.

Though I did not go up on deck because I felt so shy, I could feel the weather was beautiful. At least we met no disasters on the way. I never got to sleep but just lay there, thinking, thinking, thinking. I found the trip so long, even though the same route had been short in the past when I took it with the other school children. I began to be anxious to arrive at Fort George. I decided right there that I would never take the trip again, no matter how important it was. Ironically, it was to be my last voyage along that route.

Finally, we arrived. I came up on deck. It was still calm, the sun staying longer each day. One of the crew helped me into a canoe and we landed at the Catholic mission's anchoring beach. The same crewman carried me to the school, the school I had attended in the past. I could tell that it was the summer holiday. Nothing moved, there were not even the sounds of human voices. We came to the kitchen door of the school and entered. The first person we saw was a nun, the cook for the school, the same one who had been there a year ago, still so French in manner and speech. It was good to see her. "Minnie, avez vous malade?

Poivre, ma fille." I just nodded my head. I was feeling weak and dizzy.

She escorted me to the second floor where the dispensary was located. "Bonjour?" Another nun came out of one of the rooms, so brisk, a new one that I had never met. She had replaced the old one. The cook conversed with her. I understood everything she was telling her, that she knew me, that I had been to the school a year before. Then she left and the nurse sat me down on a chair. She disappeared and not long after I could hear the bathtub running. She came back and asked me in what language I wanted her to speak to me, Cree or French. I just shrugged my shoulders, not caring if she spoke to me or not. She just gave me a smile, an understanding smile that these nuns all seemed to have in common. After a bath, I was put to bed and asked if I wanted to eat. Yes, please. The nun seemed encouraged by my reaction and left at once for the kitchen. I lay back, my body relaxed and the motion of the ship still with me. I looked out the window beside my bed. Everything was still, and loneliness swept over me once more. I tried not to think. Then the nun returned with the father who had accompanied us when we went home with my father not long ago. He too was still the same, full of humour and teasing. "Hello, hello," he said. "Hello, Father," I replied, feeling shy that he should see me in bed. "So, you decided to come back early to go to school, eh?" he asked, still teasing. I just felt shy and looked away. Then he became serious and asked me what was wrong. Of course, I said that I did not know, not knowing where to begin. Then he became tender-faced and said that I would have lots of company later. They both left and I could hear him asking the nun many questions on the way out. I ate as much as the motion of the ship would allow me.

The nurse came back and began to examine me, asking many questions pertaining to my health. She weighed me. A year ago the other nurse had weighed me on these same scales and I had weighed then one hundred and thirty pounds, which was heavy for my height. I had always been chubby and my face round like the moon. Now the scales registered only seventy-nine pounds. I had been very sick! I had lots of company as father had promised.

Each of the nuns, brothers and the two fathers took turns visiting me everyday. I got to know the nurse; she was gentle and so patient. Her quiet manner made me feel secure. What impressed me most about this nun was her cold hands. Grandmother always believed that people with cold hands were the least painful in caring for the sick. So I told myself that I was in good hands. Indeed I was. She was not only the least painful but a very good mother. I did not have one moment of idleness under her care. She would bring me labels for medicine bottles and ask me to label them in Fort George Indian dialect. The days spent under her care were never lonely and somehow she helped to erase the memory of my departure from home.

One day she gave me the news that a doctor was coming in by plane from Moose Factory and that he would come to examine me. I explained to him about my attack. He looked at my foot, which was a bit twisted, moved it to see if I had pain, but I did not. They both looked mystified, but there was no explanation whatsoever for my situation. He never came back. After that, the nurse urged me to take walks and go outside everyday, and to come down for meals. Each day I went out for a walk, had meals, did something for the nurse in the hospital, either dusted medicine bottles or swept the dispensary. If there was nothing to do, she let me have my own idle time.

One Could Tell that They were Warriors

One day I asked if I would soon go home. The nurse must have expected that question as she explained without hesitation, "Minnie, school will start soon, you should go back to school and learn as much as you can. You have so much to give your people, you should take every advantage of learning. It won't be long before your people will need many things." I did not understand what she meant by it all, but I did not argue with her. As far as I was concerned, I was trapped. I could never get home on my own. I think she knew how I was feeling because the next day one of the fathers came up and talked to me further about staying on and going home next summer. I was in their hands so I said nothing. I put all thoughts of home in the back of my mind. As it was planned, I stayed and joined the school children when September came.

Some children were old attenders and some were new. No one was picked on, not even I. But somehow the girls seemed to have split into two groups. The new students had flown in from Point Blue, Quebec. They were Montaigne Indians, entirely different Indian children who had their own language and who spoke fluent French. The instigator, my troublesome cousin, tried to form the James Bay girls into a group to pick on the Point Blue girls. It did not work – she was astounded that she failed to get the group going. It was a very interesting situation. The old attenders knew the instigator and knew her well. When she tried anything that involved ostracism, the Point Blue girls would not take it. They retaliated and told our supervisor loudly about every little thing that happened, complaining if they did not like the way they were being treated. When they were blamed they spoke for themselves and brought out the truth. The instigator would be sent to bed early and to chapel for punishment. Dear, she looked so small and defeated. Somehow, I could not help but feel sorry for her. It's painful to watch someone who has been so aggressive be demeaned. I guess her time had to come, and this was it.

She never gave up just the same. One of the Point Blue girls and I became close friends. We did everything together – tag, hopscotch and played ball. Seeing our growing friendship, the instigator began to spread a rumour among the girls that the Point Blue girl's brother, who was also at the school, was my boyfriend. At that age having a boyfriend is rather embarrassing to some girls, and that's what she was trying to make me feel, so I would be the laughing stock of the girls. She would laugh – so ugly – trying to get the others to do the same. I took it all in, while my friend defended me, loud and clear, telling the instigator what she thought of her. Every trick the instigator tried to separate me from my friends failed. Then she would try the other way around but they fought, retaliated, stuck up for themselves and for others. One could tell that they had been warriors!

Growing Pains

During that year, I did not seem to have much interest in what I was learning. It seemed everything was repetitious and not at all challenging. I felt mixed up. My mind suddenly became aware of me. Who am I? What am I doing here? What will become of me? When will I need all this that I am learning? Everything that I did seemed to be so childish, and yet grown-up duties that I saw and did seemed to be too much. According to my culture, I was now a woman. But the routines I was expected to follow were not so womanly to me. In my culture, at that age of fourteen to sixteen, I was supposed to be married, having learned the skills and endured the duties. But here in school, I was neither a woman nor a child. I was certainly at the *makkuttuk*, the soft age, a teenager's growing pains. But as always, I survived that school year and went home for the summer.

Mighty, Fantastic and Mysterious

Once more my parents kept me back from school the year following. We summered at Old Factory and enjoyed the season's activities. The following winter, my father did not move back to Cape Hope with all the others; instead, grandmother, brother and I stayed with father at Old Factory. We were given the new warehouse that had been built that summer to live in; it was the only house available, other than the Frère store manager's and Catholic priest's home. It was part of my father's payment as he was again working in the store for the winter. We were alone but for the small winter population, and once more I was denied the familiar lands that I loved so much. I was lonely, and had only my brother to play and work with. As usual, we did not agree on everything. We did our normal chores and were not allowed to visit unless grandmother did so. I do not know why the Frère store owners could not handle the business themselves, especially during winter when there were hardly any customers around until December, when the first winter trading was possible. Their three sons were pompous show-offs who did not do any work, let alone cut wood, which my father also had to do for them. I guess they were rather spoiled, always having had servants.

Our routine was much the same as the winter we had spent on the other side of Old Factory River when both father and grandfather had worked for the Hudson's Bay Company. But something very strange arrived that winter. It was in the evening, and at that time of year it was quite dark. My father was outside our doorway, shovelling snow as there had been a heavy snowfall the previous night and our doorway was completely buried. (There was so much snow that winter that the roof of the house we were living in was level with the height of the snow. When we went out, my brother and I could walk on the roof and look down our chimney.) That evening, when father finished working, he did not come in to have his meal right away as he always did. Instead, he began to shovel the window area which was completely buried under the snow. It was dark, but he could see by the light of the moon.

We could hear him shovelling near the window, but were eager for him to finish so that we might have our meal. The shovelling slowed and then stopped, but still he did not come in. Finally, after a long silence had passed, he started banging on the window which he had just uncovered. I looked up and he motioned for me to come over. I could hear his voice, but could not understand one word. He finally just pointed towards the mouth of Old Factory River. I ran out as quickly as I could and crawled up the snow bank to stand on top with my father. I looked where he pointed and there it was, a great flashlight moving towards us. All I could imagine was the train that I had seen once at Moosonee. My mind asked, how could it get here, there is no rail. The light grew brighter and brighter. It was dark, and we could not see the body, just the light bobbing up and down on the uneven ice and snow. By this time, grandmother and brother were out watching too.

I asked father, "Sunaalunginna? What mighty, fantastic, mysterious, frightening thing is that over there?" His answer: "Qamutiaaluk," mighty, fantastic, mysterious, frightening sled. The moving light turned towards the Hudson's Bay side of Old

Factory and disappeared behind the island. We ran back in, feeling cold and chilly, as we had been standing outside without our parkas. My brother and I were so excited and could not stop talking or asking questions. We were not getting any answers, so we asked each other what it might be. Maybe it was a war plane that could not fly? Maybe a train that travelled on snow and ice? Maybe a war truck, such as we had heard about so long ago from grandfather? Maybe it was *Jamaniaaluit*, Germans?

Only Beaver Pelt Collectors

That evening we ate a tin of cooked beans and bannock that grandmother had warmed up before my father came home from work. That was another reason why we did not enjoy our stay at the post. We did not have good meals. My father had no time to hunt and he would bring home beans, tinned bologna and cans of bacon. To me, these were not food because they did not satisfy my hunger. If we got any fresh food, it was fish that grandmother caught through the ice, about a mile down the mouth of the river.

Even this was rare because grandmother too had a job to do for the store owners. She had to make dogfood for their dogs, which were tied down near the beach in front of their house. Every other night grandmother would make an outdoor fire and cook oats mixed with the leftovers gathered by the store owners. On top of that, she had to feed our dogs. This was the only time that I heard her really complain about her situation. Complain not because she had to feed the dogs, but because she felt denied her own wintering place in Cape Hope among the Inuit women. She was torn between a desire to move around with the other Inuit and to stay with father, who had been our household leader since grandfather had died. She would leave the house and announce that she had to feed the useless toy dogs. She called the store owner's dogs "useless toy dogs" because that's what they were. These people did not hunt; they were used to the food from the store. She felt that she was expected to give up all her traditional ways just so these useless dogs would be fed.

Brother and I fell asleep, full of wonders and worries about the big light. The next morning was like any other – chores, and grandmother trying to make our meaningless existence meaningful. Brother and I kept looking for the big light all morning. After father came home for lunch, we saw it across the frozen river but with no lights on. It was a snowmobile. It looked so small compared to what I had pictured in my mind. I was disappointed! Though it fascinated me – how does it move without dogs? – I wondered who would travel with something like that. It came closer, but brother and I were not allowed to go near as grandmother said that it was *qallunaraaluit* – big, important, avaricious. So we stood outside of the house and watched, trying to find out who was on it. The snowmobile stopped in front of the store; there were two *qallunaaq* men and one woman. Brother and I recognized one man, as we had seen him every summer when he came to collect beaver pelts from the Indians.

Nobody Told Me that I had to Grow Strange

Our lives went on in the same routine day in and day out, get up, eat, cut wood, get pails of water, do chores inside, play and occupy fingers, and fight with brother. But at this time I began to notice that something awful was happening to me. I had never noticed it in other women, at least I never thought to look for it in other women. I had never been told that I would grow into a different shape; I began to worry and wondered what was happening to me. My chest seemed to grow. I was growing hairs where I thought I should have no hair. I began to have cramps in my stomach for no reason. I would lay in bed and listen to father's and grandmother's snores at night and wonder what was happening. I would decide that I would be the only one who will look strange! That I will be the only one who will have hairs in odd places. I would get scared and cry silently. I would dream about the priest in Fort George, standing in the doorway with his big, black beard, laughing his head off at me, and wake up so unhappy. I did not tell anyone. If grandmother noticed or knew, she did not say anything about it.

I felt so unhappy that I did my chores with no interest. I was so occupied with myself that nothing else mattered. Whenever I spoke, my words seemed to be sharp, especially to my brother. He seemed to be the only one who noticed that I was unhappy. "Sullutuaalussalirpit? What is the matter with you?" Obviously he was much bothered by the unpleasantness I was creating by not seeming to care about my chores. Did he accept this strange way of growing better than I did? Or did boys and men just naturally accept growing strange? Did they grow strange at all? No one was there to tell me all about it, so it became something else I had to get used to, to accept as another trial to be endured.

Certainly It was a Time of Joy

December arrived and grandmother told brother and me to start looking towards the mouth of the river, to see if the traders were coming. That gave me an exciting lift and made me forget about myself for awhile. It was good to see all our relatives again and to have playmates for a while. Christmas was coming too, the time when every Inuit went to the missionaries to receive gifts for the children, a practise of the missionaries for years. Every child had to bring a little handmade bag with his or her name sewn on it before they left for their wintering place, and we would pick them up around this time of year. The bags would be bulging with candy, gum, chocolate and a small toy.

Everyday we would look for the traders. By this time my brother and I were more skilled in how to look at the horizon, and we could recognize what we were looking for. Then one evening, father came in and announced that the qimussiit, the dog teams, could be heard. We all went out to listen, and sure enough, in the still of the night, we could hear the breathing of the dogs mixed with the swish of feet and the crunching sound of the hard snow, every now and then a man urging the dogs to go faster. What a beautiful sound that was to my ears. Then we could see their dark movements, and father began to call the dogs, aho aho aho, until they stopped right in front of the house.

The women and children came in all at once. I should say,

they all came sliding into the porch, because our door was like a hole in a den. Everybody was talking, handshaking, nose caressing, relations being strengthened, brother and I being noticed. There was so much excitement that evening. Every woman had a bundle of seal meat for grandmother, all the special parts of the seal that these women knew she liked. Even her *arnaliak*, bring-her-to-be-a-woman, brought her some braided seal intestines which she had prepared herself. The excitement died down after a big meal of boiled seal meat, fresh bannock and hot tea. That, too, was much welcomed, the meat that warmed up the insides and brought the natural sweat to the skin. Men began to talk, each one taking a turn, and describing what kind of hunt they had had during the fall, how many tracks of fox were seen, and how many each had caught so far. One by one the children were falling asleep, and the women began to make out a place to sleep for each family. By the time everybody was under his covers, the floor could not be seen, everybody was in bed. It was a time of joy to be all together again.

To Become a Woman is even Stranger

With all the snoring going on, brother and I were still awake. We took the opportunity to stay up as long as we could while no one noticed in all the excitement and talk. Grandmother finally came to straighten out our bed – *piluijartuq*, taking off the loose furs of caribou. The word originated with the caribou skins that had been used for mattresses, though now our mattresses were made of cloth and stuffed with eider-down feathers. In any event, this is what she did after she had made sure that everything was in order and the stove off. This is one chore she did without fail, to make sure the fire was out in case there should be a wind in the middle of the night that might blow the sparks inwards from the chimney and set fire to the house. She was not taking any chances as the house was not hers, and she felt responsible if there should be any damage. It is another of our traditions, not to damage someone else's property, not to stay in an empty house, even if we should enter when there is nobody in, not to take to keep, if borrowing, any item or equipment, not to pick up something that was left behind by its owner.

Earlier, in the middle of the excitement, I had noticed that I passed water every time I did something a little strenuous. It puzzled me, so I went to grandmother and asked her why I did that. She had looked at me rather pained and sympathetic and ordered me to say no more, because I had asked her loudly in front of all these people. I did not think anyone had heard me, at least no one turned around. Then I forgot all about it and I guess she did, too.

I sat on a chair while grandmother fixed our bed. There was not a sound, only a few people dozing off. I felt itchy on my leg, on the inside of my thigh, so I decided to investigate. I pulled my dress up, and turned the legs of my bloomers inside out. I was so occupied trying to see what was on my skin that I failed to notice my bloomers. All of a sudden, my brother burst out laughing with all his innocent might, "Ha, ha, ha! My sister has excrement in her bloomers! Ha, ha, ha!" I pulled down my dress so fast, not because I believed what he said, but because I realized he had been watching me. I sat there stunned. Grandmother said, "Nauk? Let's see?" So I showed her while brother curled up with laughter, no doubt pleased that he had found something else to pick on me about. I became curious and looked more intensely. Sure, it did look like dung, but I didn't, I didn't do it! There was something there, dark, dry and flaking. Grandmother examined me closely and ordered me to bed.

At this point father forced his drowsy voice and said, "Sualussalippitik? What are you two doing at this odd hour?" and he turned towards the wall and went back to sleep. A few heads looked up and turned our way. Grandmother dimmed the lamp. She did not turn it right off as there were a couple of mothers with babies, and they might need the light to nurse them in the middle of the night. I lay awake and wondered what was happening to me, and began to cry silently. I could feel grandmother was not asleep as she was right next to me. When brother fell asleep, she reached gently down under our bed, and pulled out the wooden box in which we kept our clean clothing. She took out my bloomers and a pair of thick pants which she usually wore under her dress when we travelled in the winter. She ordered me to put them on and asked me to go to sleep.

The next morning, there was hustle and bustle all around, but more calm than the previous night. When I awoke I remembered my situation and, burying my head under the covers, began to cry. I pretended to be asleep when anyone came near. All my concerned aunts and my father kept coming over to ask if I was sick. I did not answer. I had enough questions of my own to think about. Suddenly I could hear my outspoken aunt asking, why isn't Minnie up and out looking at the world? Nobody answered. Of course, she became more curious. As no one was answering, she became louder and louder. I uncovered my head and began to watch her as she walked back and forth in the middle of the floor. Grandmother finally said to her, "Let's go outside," and out they went. In a few minutes they came back in and with tears in her eyes, my aunt came over to me and gave me the deepest love sounds she had ever expressed to me. I wondered more than ever what was happening to me. Nothing else was said for a few minutes. Everybody seemed to think deep in their own thoughts.

Nobody was telling me anything, and I had no idea how to question them about it. I went back under my covers and sobbed silently. Then I heard my father giving me love sounds, so deep and concerned that I stopped sobbing. I opened my eyes, not uncovering my head. Father urged me to stay in bed as long as I wanted. Has something happened to me that is known to everybody? Have I reached some important point of life? Nobody told me anything, but their concerned and sympathetic treatment told me that something had happened to me that was nothing new to them.

During the day everybody was getting ready to go trading. Grandmother had planned to go with the women to the Hudson's Bay store and to Frère's, not to mention visiting the missionaries and some Indian families that were around the post. But grandmother did not go, she and I were the only ones who stayed behind. Even brother was taken by one of our aunts, and father went to work. When grandmother and I were alone, she began to talk to me. "Minnie, this is not play, it is serious. You have entered into womanhood. This will happen to you now every month. You have to tell me when it happens so I can fix something for you to wear. It will come to you every month, unless, of course, a man has touched you, then it will stop. Every woman has it." I understood what she said and felt relieved; in fact, I felt proud. I kept telling myself that I was now a woman, not a little girl anymore, and I began to watch the other women and noticed their chests. They looked like me, I assured myself.

I was much relieved, though still one thing bothered me — about a man touching me. I asked myself if this meant any man. Did it mean I would no longer caress my father with my nose? Did it mean that I would no longer sit on the laps of my uncles? What about my brother? Did he count as a man or just a boy, and what about all my other boy cousins with whom I played tag and went sliding? They were all men; could I not let them touch me anymore? And why will I not bleed, as my grandmother put it, if a man touches me? I did not dare ask these questions, so I left them there in my mind. What bothered me most was, how can I bleed automatically and stop bleeding automatically without doing anything? It certainly was strange to grow into womanhood!

One Drains Blood to Grow Up

Grandmother reached down again under our bed and pulled out our clean clothes box and handed me another pair of clean bloomers. She reached further under our bed and pulled out a burlap sack full of moss, moss earth that is used to diaper babies. I felt I had grown both ways, to womanhood and back to baby days. It seemed grandmother was well-prepared for this event. Now when I thought of it, I had seen her taking pieces of wood out of this moss last summer, and I had thought it was for my new baby cousins. She showed me how to fix a piece of rag and wrap this moss inside, and how to fit it onto myself. She told me never to leave it around, especially outside where the dogs could get at it, that I should not allow the dogs to eat my blood or I would encourage them to crave for human blood. She told me that I should always put them in the fire discreetly, like a woman should, as she put it. Her last advice was that I should never discuss it with my little girlfriends, that they would laugh at me if I did. I was now a woman, and it was my very own affair. I felt elated and so grown-up; I felt proud that I was categorized as a woman.

The traders all came back and there was much bustle all over again. I, too, joined in the excitement but I felt very aware of my situation. I sat near grandmother, who was dishing out seal meat for each family. I was supposed to be learning how to serve food on individual plates, but instead I sat looking at every woman, thinking. Imagine, every one of them has to put up with this uncomfortable diaper every month, and yet they do not complain. How patient they are. How can they resist talking about it when it is such a novelty? None of them show discomfort when they walk. . . . Grandmother woke me out of my thoughts by asking me to take father's plate to him. Then she called the others to take theirs to their own families. Grandmother allowed me to have some tea. It was an adult treat, and usually I practically had to beg for some. Now that I was free to have all I wanted, I did not really like it. I asked for my usual gravy, and grandmother said, "Help yourself." She began to treat me like an adult. My body felt drained of all its blood.

Adults are Disappointed Too

The traders left to return to Cape Hope Island or to wherever they were wintering. Our family went back to its routine, but something was added to my little sewing box. Father made me a box of my own, to store my own clothing in, instead of having them in with grandmother's and brother's things. I felt so proud, and everyday I opened the box and arranged the contents over and over. Grandmother never complained about it, and she just let me go on, as long as my duties were done. Father sometimes sat on

149

his bed, and I would realize that he was watching me. He would have on his face an approving smile and give me a loving sound. It seemed that overnight I was allowed to do things in my own way. Sometimes I enjoyed the sudden change of attitude, and sometimes I felt confused. I was not reminded over and over that my duties came first. I could play before or after. I could drink tea if I wanted, I could help myself instead of being given something that I did not want. I felt that I was suddenly released from everything that at one time I had thought was such a heavy duty.

I received my usual bag of candies from the missionaries for Christmas. The bag seemed childish after all; the adults did not receive them. Every year my brother and I fought over our bags, comparing who got what. Now I was giving some of my candy to him, which he took gladly. I did not feel like hiding them under my pillow in case he took some out behind my back. I just left the bag there on the table. I did not feel like fighting over them. It was funny, my brother did not touch them either, now that they were all out in the open.

The new year months, January, February and March arrived, and my novelty did not come. I began to ask grandmother, "I thought you said that I would get it every month?" "Not for a while. Sometimes it will not come, until it paces right for you," she said. Well, that I did not understand, but her attitude told me not to talk about it any further, so I let it be. We were quiet. But somehow grandmother could always see right through me and said, "You don't suddenly will everything to happen for you, just because you are an adult now. Disappointments also come to adults; it is up to you how you take them."

Bad Times are Sometimes Good Luck

One day father came home from work early, acting very mad. His right cheek, under his eye, was bleeding. All he said was, "They do not know how to play or how to lose like adults." He was very angry. We were all dumbfounded, as we had never seen him like that before.

He was moving around hurriedly, and ordered grandmother to pack. We did not dare ask him anything. We packed and packed. Finally, he slowed down and spoke: "We do not have to stay here, they do not deserve my services, it is not worth it to have the children lonely for the sake of people like that. We will leave first thing tomorrow morning and join the Cape Hope Islanders." We did not ask any questions, not when he was so mad. I looked at my brother. His eyes were dancing, trying to hide a happy smile. Even grandmother's movements were joyous. I guess that was the best news we had heard since Christmas. Father ordered us to go to bed early and rise early in the morning, so that we might leave before dawn and reach Cape Hope before dark. We did so, gladly.

Next morning, grandmother was warming the food when we awoke, and father was already dressed. Brother and I forced ourselves to get up and act normally. We ate and brought all our belongings to the sled which father was then hitching, and we helped him to harness the dogs. The dogs looked surprised as they had hardly worked all winter. We left the post. I looked back as we passed out of the mouth of the Old Factory River. I could see that no one was up, the whole island looked still and cold. I looked around me, to the horizon. Everything was snowy. The sun was barely up but I could tell it was going to be a beautiful day.

Our dogs were slow, and some kept glancing back towards our sled, pressing father to command them. One could tell they had not been worked. They seemed to be glad when father urged them on. Halfway to Cape Hope we stopped for hot tea and frozen bannock. The dogs never bothered to fool around; they were tired, and all took a nap.

After tea, father and brother combed the traces. The word "combed" we use when men untangle the traces. No one had to bring out the whip, as not one dog got up during the combing. Usually one of them will try to run away during this process. A dog bolting from the team can cause all the others to run, too. That could be dangerous for travellers, if they are left by the dogs when they are nowhere near home, far from the settlements. It has happened to inexperienced travellers. Men have walked all the way home, leaving their belongings, when this happened to them. It has happened, too, to experienced travellers who were just a little careless. People have to be ready at all times to run after a dog that is running away, to make sure that the others do not follow. The sled has to be lashed at all times while the men comb the traces.

While father and brother were busy, grandmother and I were sitting on the sled, whispering so we wouldn't excite the dogs. I could tell grandmother was trying to make conversation, to prevent me from asking what had happened at Frère stores the previous night, and I was dying to know.

When we were all set after tea and untangling, father urged the dogs to go. Some were willing to run, some were doped with sleep, finally all fell into an even pace. It was high noon now, and the landmarks began to look familiar. There was the area where father had gone camping with the other couples when mother became sick. There was the island where we picked seagull eggs every spring. Just beyond that was Cape Hope Island. What a pretty site!

We arrived before dark. Everybody came down to meet us. Father looked so relieved. All the men were around him, shaking hands. News was being exchanged. Grandmother, brother and I were brought to our aunt, and fed with good warming food. All the men helped father to unharness the dogs, to bring in our gear, and put away his equipment. It was so good to be there among familiar people. We did not bother to settle into our house as we had just arrived in time for the move to the goose hunt at Charlton Island. We stayed with our aunt, crowded but nice and warm with people we knew well to talk to.

Though I was happy again to be among friendly faces, I still had not forgotten about father's sudden departure from Old Factory. It was not like him to leave his responsibilities. In the past he had preached to brother and me to look after our responsibilities well and to the bitter end. I had never known father to talk about his problems, his worries, or his joys to grandmother. If he wanted to discuss his personal feelings, it was with one of my aunts. In a couple of days our aunt told us what had happened at Frère stores.

Apparently father had been playing checkers with the younger son of the owner, and father had been winning the game. The younger boy did not take it as a game, he got mad, and started a fistfight with father. Father did not take it and fought back, which made the boy madder. He went at father and pushed him right against a wall, catching his eyelid on a nail where a calendar hung. No wonder he came home so mad, puffing like an old walrus. People could not understand why some parents would allow a young boy to fight an adult. That was unheard of. Everybody was glad that father had left. They, the Frères, did not deserve his services, that was the agreement in our camp. That was the news, and it was forgotten after that. So, it was bad times for the Frères, but good luck for brother and me to be among the people we knew so well.

Innocent Woman

After a couple of days, when everybody was ready for the trip, we left early one morning for Charlton Island. It was March month, and the ice and snow were glistening and shimmering in the sun. We camped at the usual place, a site that my people have visited since the late 1800s when grandfather Weetaltuk first found these hunting and camping areas. It was then 1951. Men stocked basking seals, while women worked on the skins. Children hunted ptarmigan and rabbits and gathered spruce gum.

Each day the sun was hotter, the snow was melting fast. Grandmother, brother and I visited grandfather Symma's grave. We could see the mark on the tree which by now was seeping sap. Some other visitors had already dug the snow to make sure the cross was standing upright. No matter who they were or how close they had been to her, grandmother always felt it a duty to visit graves. She would take me with her, if anyone had died while I was away at school. From her, I know whose grave is where. They are scattered on little islands, deep in the woods, and some in the valleys. Some have no crosses and some do; none bear the names of the dead, but I know who they are, what they were

153

like and how I was related to them. Each year she visited Symma's grave, and she accepted his death a little more, with less pain. By this time, too, he had a namesake, my aunt's newborn son. Grandmother called the baby *aipa*, partner, mate or husband. Symma's soul rested in peace in its grave. She now had someone to talk to, the way she used to talk to Symma.

Towards the April month, we all moved southeast of Charlton to the goose hunt. At this time, I suddenly remembered about my novelty. It had not come at all. I thought back, trying to figure out what man had touched me. Father had caressed me with his nose many times, I had gone sliding with my boy cousins and all my uncles caressed my nose when we arrived at Cape Hope. Yes, I assured myself, I have certainly been touched by many men. Yes, they have all stopped my novelty from coming again. I was, indeed, an innocent woman!

Brother Was Growing Too

We did our usual goose hunting and returned to Cape Hope to wait for the spring season to turn into summer. It was the most beautiful spring we had ever had. There was hardly any rain and the sun shone and shone. It was as if nature was saying, "Had a lot of snow this winter, now I must hurry to melt it away." The ice, along with our sled tracks, melted without any help from the winds. People were getting ready to move to Old Factory. This year we decided that everybody would go, in a way to see each other off, as Weetaltuk had never stayed at the post. He went back after trading for a couple of days. The ones that stayed netted fish, hunted ducks and welcomed the school children and ships. Father navigated as usual.

Brother and I fought, but sometimes I ignored him when I remembered that I was growing up. That summer, father gave him permission to use his motor and the canoe if he needed it. Brother was very careful and did not dare waste gas or motor oil. The only time he used it was to check the nets or to go and meet the ships down at the mouth of Old Factory River. He never had anyone to bring back to the settlement but he always came back with news, and always he had an orange or apple that the crew had given him. He would share the two fruits among our little cousins.

One evening, brother had gone out to check the nets. He took some time to come back. It was getting dark. Grandmother and I waited, and every now and then we would look for him from our doorway. We kept listening for his motor, as every motor had a different sound, and we always knew who was coming by their sound, even if we did not see them near. Grandmother thought that perhaps there were no fish in our nets, so maybe brother was visiting instead of coming right home as he often did, just so grandmother would not be disappointed with his empty hands. Brother had been very close to our grandmother. He had never hurt her feelings or disobeyed her wishes. He always seemed to know how to cope and take care of her in our crises. If he knew ahead of time that there would be some sadness, disappointment or bad news, he always tried to prevent them before grandmother knew. Sometimes he was successful, other times grandmother found out before he could do anything. The worst thing that could happen, what made grandmother most unhappy, was the destruction of father's equipment. Grandmother would have to do some painful explaining for it. It was she who was blamed for what we ruined, she was the one who was responsible for seeing that brother and I followed father's rules while he was away.

That evening brother came in, acting as though nothing had happened. In fact he looked pleased. His pleased look made me suspicious and very curious. He kept on smiling while he was eating, probably trying to find words to explain his lateness. Neither grandmother nor I questioned him, for we believed that if a person is questioned or forced to explain themselves, they will only lie. I sat there, dying from curiosity and dying to ask him a few questions. Grandmother had warned me before he came home that I should not do so, that I should act normal. That was very hard to do. As usual, grandmother could see right through me. I was itching to get at brother. But she knew what to do. She was sewing a pair of kamiit for an Indian. She asked me to fix the sinew threads, so she could just thread them to her needle when she wanted one. Brother kept on eating, grandmother sewed, and I was now busy with something else. That made me forget my urge to ask questions. Bedtime came, and we all went out to relieve ourselves, and then climbed into our eider-down blankets.

Grandmother was already sewing when I awoke the next morning, and brother was nowhere around. I got dressed and went out to look at the world. Seagulls were flying above the nets, birds were singing, and the river in front of our settlement was shimmering in the sun. It was calm, deep blue. I went back in and fed myself with the oats that grandmother had left on our stove. I asked her where brother was, and she said that he had gone down to check our canoe, to see that it was safe in case something had happened during the night.

Grandmother finished the *kamiit*. I could see that she was tired from sitting so long. She asked me to put on the fire outside and make tea; she was going to visit for awhile and went out. She was not going far, just next-door to my aunt's, probably to empty the thoughts that she had been gathering over the last two days while sewing and fixing skins, and also to catch up on what had been happening next-door.

I made the fire and filled the kettle of water to make tea. Brother came back and the first thing he asked was: "where is our *anana*?" That is what we called our grandmother — mother. I told brother where she was, and he sat down near the fire where I was waiting for the kettle to boil. He bagan to talk and sort of asked me, "Would you tell anyone why I was late coming home last night?" I could feel that he did not really trust me. I did not look at him, but just pretended to fix the fire. I was thinking: shall I ask him or just give him the trust that I will not tell? I could easily use whatever he was about to tell me to retaliate the next time he picked on me. I gave him the trust.

He began. "When I came back from the nets, I was late because I had to take apart the whole motor. I dropped it in the water when I was trying to take it off the canoe to put it back in the shed. After I fished it out, I took every screw, bolt and little wire, and dried every piece with my shirt, and put it back together." I could not believe my ears. Father would find out, and would he and grandmother get it! I asked him, does it work? "Yes, it works. I tried it after, did you not hear the motor over and over last night?" No, I had not heard it, nor had grandmother. Probably it was a good thing that we had not heard it, because we could tell the sound of a motor running on land, as well as in the water. I asked brother, "How did you know how to take it apart and put it back together again?" He said, "I have watched father, I have seen the insides of motors many times, and I had memorized every piece, where it goes, as I took it out. Please, don't tell grandmother, she might tell father."

I felt *naalinnk*, love and sympathy for him. Momentarily, I put myself in his mind and thought how he felt. I felt fear for him in case the motor did not work in the future. I agreed that I would not tell, ever. I looked at him as he got up to enter our tent. Poor little brother, he is growing and can take a motor apart and put it back together like a man. It is true that he always watched father when he was fixing something or working on any equipment, like motors or watches. I gave him the trust and to this day neither father nor grandmother knows it ever happened. It has been a longtime secret between the two of us. The motor did work all that summer, and father had it for a few more years until he decided to get one of a higher horse power. Then he gave it to brother when brother began to go hunting on his own.

After that, our relationship began to change. We gave each other more secrets and talked about our father and grandmother. But we never talked about their good sides, only what we thought to be their bad sides. We no longer fought over our duties, but talked about our only two close relatives, how much work they wanted us to do, how we always had to control ourselves for them, how they always wanted us to look after our responsibilities well. We were growing physically but not so well mentally. But I noticed that brother was growing, too.

Still an Innocent

The school ships arrived again and I went back to Fort George. At the school, some changes had been made. There was a new hospital that had been added to the school. The nurse with the cool hands was still there. The girls had a new supervisor who spoke perfect Cree. There was a new cook and one new brother. There were more servants, more new Point Blue children and more Indian children from the area surrounding Fort George. The instigator was not there.

Before the school year started, the priest who was the head principal asked me to come to his office. He told me that I would have to repeat grade eight, because the grades did not go beyond that at Fort George, that to continue I would have to go away somewhere else. He gave me an alternative: that I should do it and if I did not like it, I would go to work around or by Christmas time. He asked me if my father would object to that. Father had no idea what was happening, least of all that I was going to work instead of learning. He had no idea about *qallunaat* gradings at school. The priest said that he could write and ask him about it. But father would not receive the letter before Christmas; he had gone to where they wait for freeze-up. So I told the priest that I thought he would not object, though I was not even sure myself. To me it sounded more challenging to go to work than to repeat what I had already learned.

Before school started, we all took a bath in a tub behind a curtain in the girls' playroom. While each girl was in the tub, the supervisor came in to make sure they were washing right. My turn came and the nun came in. She could see that I was washing right, but pretended to help me. I could tell that she had things to say because she was not washing me properly. After sizing me up, she began to ask, "Did you menstruate yet?" I did not know what she meant by menstruate and I told her so. She began again, "Did you bleed down there yet?" Yes. "When was the last time?" My first and last time was in December. "Oh, mon Dieu! Did any man or boy touch you?" Yes, yes, many times. "Oh, mon Dieu! Where?" Here and here, and I pointed to my back, my legs, wherever I remembered that father, uncles or boy cousins had touched me. "And you have not bled since?" No.

I answered her questions very matter-of-factly, full of innocence. How could I know that she had other things in mind, things that were not known to me? She ordered me to keep washing and ran out very excited. I could hear all the girls through the curtain getting a bit noisier, because she had run in the direction of the hospital. A few moments later she came back in, more calmly, and ordered me to dress. When all the girls had bathed, it was suppertime, and we all lined up to walk quietly to the dining room. The rules were the same as they had always been.

The next day, first thing in the morning after breakfast, our supervisor took me to the hospital and brought me into the examining room. I had not been in this new section. She asked me to sit and wait for the nurse, the same nurse that had impressed me with her cool hands. By now she was not just a nurse, but a doctor. I did not know why I had to be seen by her. I wondered if I was sick without knowing or feeling it myself. What will she do to me? Will she use all this equipment that looks so fantastic? Will I be in pain? I shivered. Finally, I could hear the swish of her long, white gown coming to the dispensary. I had not seen her since I had arrived. She was the same — tender-voiced, gentle and with cool hands, such a kindly face, and a smile that warmed you up. I must have looked scared as she assured me not to be afraid. She spoke to me as she was examining me all over, some Cree, some English, and some French.

Then she began to ask, "Have you ever been touched by a man?" Yes. "Minnie, I do not mean touched with a finger, or with your body against any man. What I mean by touch is when you and a man have intercourse." I was bewildered, and she could probably see that, and so she went on: "You see, Minnie, intercourse is when a man puts his penis into your vagina." I was more bewildered. "You see, Minnie, when that happens, a woman can get pregnant." More bewildered. "You see, Minnie, when a woman gets pregnant, it means that she will have a baby growing in her stomach."

How was I to know that she was telling me the truth? Throughout all my growing years, I had been told by grandmother that all my little cousins arrived by dog team, that someone found them while they were away cutting wood, that everybody decided who to give them to. Some had *alluk*, a seal hole, on the floor where these cousins had come out to be taken by their mothers. Grandmother proved it so, pointing out that the hole in our floor in Cape Hope was such a one. It was a hole where a knot-hole of the tree had been cut along with the board. My brother and I had loosened it to play, pretending that it was a seal hole. Grandmother had always made us cover the hole for her own reasons — the wind blew in, or mice might get into the house — but she told us that we should not play with it because that is where brother and I came out to go to our mother and father. If another baby should come in through that hole, nobody would be ready to keep it, that we would be responsible if a baby came when nobody was ready to have one, that she was too old now, and that brother and I were too young, that father did not have a wife, and that all the other people who could have one already had one. She never told us anything about sex or intercourse, even though we had been well-prepared with what she considered essential for marriage, as far as duties were concerned. I know now that it was the boys who were taught when they reached an age, the time to know about sex, not the girls. The girls would learn from their *angilissiat* when the time came. I had not reached that stage. I was utterly confused and did not know who to believe.

The nun went on, "You see, Minnie, you do not do this until you are married," Do people do things other than attend to their duties when they are married? I understood her words, but not what she meant. "Did you have nice holidays at home?" Yes. "Minnie, have you been sick in the mornings?" No. "Do you want to eat more than you usually do?" I did not know and I had not noticed. "Does your chest itch?" No. "You have not had intercourse with a man, have you?" No, I do not know and I do not understand. Poor nun, how she must have felt at that moment! When I think back on that episode, I realize that she was probably caught by many things in her mind, as much as I was. She was afraid to give too much information about sex when she was not sure how much I knew. Little did she know that she gave me more information than I had received from anyone. At least she made me wonder what goes on with married couples. Somehow she had to find out if I had been touched by a man and was pregnant. She examined me, the way doctors examine pregnant women, then ordered me to get up and dress. "You are fine," she said, "there is nothing wrong with you. You will bleed again, you have to, all girls do at a certain age, and you are at that age." Well, grandmother had told me that. But why had it not come back? Nobody knew, least of all me.

I went back to the girls' room, and our supervisor asked me if the doctor had explained or told me anything. I said yes, without much interest, because I did not really understand. It was so vague, it sounded so mysterious, and a bit frightening. (I swear on the solid ground I walk on today that my daughter will know everything.) The supervisor ran over to the hospital, and all the girls went wild and noisy. She came back, looking very much relieved. I was still an innocent.

The Sick Gave Me Strength

School began but I was very bored. The thought of work was challenging and attractive to me, especially when I saw that the employees received different treatment from the others. They had work to do. They could go to the store once a week. They could go for walks when they had finished work. They sat at the back of the chapel. They were much more involved with other things, while the school children went to bed early and conformed to the rules. They wore the clothing they wanted, not what was passed on to them from others. Some of them changed everyday. Most of the time I wondered where I would be put to work. Will it be in the kitchen? Laundry? Father-house? Or the new hospital?

At the end of November our school pictures were taken. They would be framed and hung in the girls' and boys' rooms. The same pictures were always sent home to the local priest's house to be hung in his living room where the parents would see them when they came to visit. After mine was taken, I was told that another would have to be shot. This time I was given something to wear against my skin and across my chest. I called it my harness. The nun explained to me that I did not look nice with my chest showing too much, and that I had to wear this to flatten it. It was painful, and it hurt me all over my chest. My breathing was very uncomfortable, but I sat and posed as I was directed. Once again, we were shown our pictures, but my chest was still too obvious to the nuns. It seemed school girls should not have chests growing normally. Believe me, the nuns were as old-fashioned as my grandmother. My picture was given to me instead of being hung, and I sent it to my father.

The next day, the priest asked me and another Indian girl who was also repeating grade eight to see him in his office. She and I were good friends. He began by saying, "The kitchen and the hospital need extra help, and I think you two are a bit grown to be with the children. You will be paid five dollars a month. The sister will make arrangements for you to move in with the servants." That was that. My friend was put to work in the kitchen and I was sent to help at the hospital.

As there were more school children that year, there were more servants, more employees. All of them had something to do. Three were in the kitchen, one at the father-house plus the laundry, and one seemed to be all over the place. I suppose she was there to give a hand wherever the work was lagging behind. My friend was the extra helper in the kitchen, in the laundry and at the father-house. The day I began to work at the hospital, the nun doctor showed me around. The building itself was long with a corridor in the middle and rooms on both sides. There were eleven patient rooms, one kitchen, the doctors' room, linen room, X-ray room and adjoining film developing room, an office for the doctor, dispensary, and operating room.

There were four patients in the hospital when I started to work. One was a retarded, half-blind Indian girl from Great Whale River. She had been there for a long time, as I had seen her when I first came to the school. She was bedridden before the nun doctor came, but now she was walking. She walked up the stairs to the chapel. She knew all the hymns and prayers by heart having heard them over and over; the dispensary was right next door to the chapel. She understood when she was spoken to, but could not talk back. During her years in bed she had put on so much weight that she had more difficulty in lifting herself than in walking. That much I knew about her. I could see there was no way she could ever go home, not if her parents were hunters who had to travel back and forth to hunt beaver. My heart went out to her. How much she must be in pain. I called her "the clever one" in her language. It amazed me that she always knew who it was who came into her room, that her gestures showed her under-standing when she was spoken to.

Another patient was a baby, a year and a half old, also re-tarded. I was not sure if she was really retarded, but I could see that her whole body had no strength, and her head constantly swayed around from the neck. The nun had started to put her in a baby walker with wheels, until she could push herself around. Every morning one of us would put her "on wheels," and let her out into the corridor. She was from Fort George and her parents came to see her everytime they came back from the bush. My heart went out to her, too.

There was also a two-year-old boy. Though nothing seemed to be wrong with him, he suffered from some internal disorder. He was very mischievous and got into all sorts of distresses. We had to watch him extra carefully; in fact, he made things happen at the hospital. Sometimes he made the nun and I so mad, other times we couldn't help but laugh at the things he did.

The fourth patient was an Indian man. I had known this man ever since I had come to Fort George. He was the janitor at the school. For as long as I could remember, everybody made fun of him, yet no matter how much ridicule he was confronted with, he never answered, never fought back, just kept on with his work. I could see that he had a lot on his mind. People in the community said that he was not married because he was not wanted by anyone as a son-in-law, least of all by any woman. Some said that he did things that were not normal, and all the adults in the community had managed to scare their children with him. Sometimes I used to hear the Fort George children say that he was crazy, and that was how he was known in their community. I left Fort George without ever finding out what was wrong with him medically. Now, he was here, in this hospital, confined and chained to his bed. The chain was just long enough for him to reach the toilet and to allow him to get up and around his bed.

The nun showed me what I had to do everyday and what routine to follow to get the work done. I had to rise at 7:00 A.M., attend the chapel service with everybody else, have breakfast, then leave like all the other servants who had work to do. For a week, the nun stayed with me to show me what had to be done, and eventually I was on my own, learning to make my own decisions. I would bring meals and medicine to my clever one, and to the little boy, who knew how to eat on his own. The nun and I took turns feeding the baby. She did not let me take the man's tray to him for about a week. She took it to him herself, or some days she would take me with her. She always knocked at his door first, before she opened it. Some days he would be sitting on his bed, some days he would be dancing, sweat dripping down his face. Some days he just smiled. Some days he said something like good, good. The nun would watch us, probably studying our reactions. She watched me the most, trying to find out if I was scared, and I was. I would try to hide my fear; after all, I had known him when he was free in the world. I would gather all my strength and act a little braver. When we got out of the room, the nun would pat my shoulders. The day she decided to let me take the man's tray by myself, she made me a nurse's cap. She felt it would help the man see that there was some authority. He tended to grab our arms, and he would try to terrorize us if we did not wear our uniforms. If we went into his room wearing our white uniforms, however, he was passive and obedient.

I put on the cap, and she spoke, "You know, Minnie, you should think seriously about nursing, you have all the capabilities. You are patient, you are pleasant. But there is one thing you have to have, which you could learn to have with training, and that is mental strength, to be able to cope with pain without fainting. Can you see what could happen to a patient while you were busy fainting?" I could not help but smile at her, as I have been trained by my people to have a sense of humour when fear is at hand. So, I said, "The patient would probably die while I was on the verge of collapse." That she took seriously, and said, "You see, Minnie, you have the right attitude, all the more that you should be a nurse."

She was feeding the baby, standing with her back to me while talking, opening up my mind, putting there wishes and hopes that I might be as knowledgeable as she. I stood there for some time, leaning against the counter of the kitchen sink. I looked at her and wondered if she was serious. Did she mean that an Inuk can become a nurse, too? I thought only qallunaat could do that. How would I go about wanting to be a nurse? Where would I have to go to learn such things? The questions bothered me but the idea sounded challenging. I sized her up. She was always so helpful and so willing to share her knowledge and easy to talk to. I began to ask her the questions I had in mind. She explained, "Minnie, if you are serious, arrangements could be made for you to go to Ottawa with the sisters. The sisters have a big hospital there. Now? No, it would have to be next summer. Where would you stay? They have places for girls like you. But you do not have to wait till then, you could begin here, right here, in this hospital. We have all the equipment and you have the grades that are necessary to learn. If you start here, you could continue down there. Sometimes we don't have much to do here, and when you have some spare time, you could read the anatomy books. You think about it, and let me know."

Our daily jobs were never dull, there was always something to be done. When the patients finished breakfast, I made and changed their beds, cleaned the bathrooms, dusted and swept the whole hospital. As she promised, she taught me anatomy names; some sounded like Inuit words and were easy to memorize, others I had to go over and over. No matter how busy she was, she would have me repeat the anatomy names when we were alone together. She would take me into the X-ray room and show me how to use and develop films, how to handle them in the darkroom, how to mind the timer so the films wouldn't be ruined. I liked the X-raying most because the machine fascinated me, and the more it fascinated me, the more curious about it I became. One day she asked me to X-ray a six-year-old boy from the school. He was not feeling well in his stomach. I lined up the machine, put in the film, asked the boy to stand against it and take a deep breath. I clicked the button. I asked the boy to wait, and went into the darkroom to process the film. The nun was in her office, and I told her that I was finished. She came and looked at the film. When she put it against the light, all I could think was, is that how we look? The shapes of the bones were the same as the pictures in the anatomy book. How did the person who wrote the book know all this? I did not ask, I just listened to her and began to trust her more.

Then I had to sterilize all the equipment in the operating room. I had to wear rubber gloves to handle them. I did not like that, my imagination would go wild with all those sharp instruments. Would I have to use these on human bodies? I would shiver, and get on with the work. I hated that room.

The month of February arrived. Indians began to come to the hospital with heavy colds, complaining of pains in their chests. There was flu again. In just a few weeks, every bed in the hospital was occupied. There was more work. I had to be with the nun constantly. I could not even take my daily walk outdoors, except to bring the laundry to the laundry house. Some nights we would be up so late, trying to keep up with the work. There were more temperatures to be taken, read, and recorded, more bed pans to be washed, more beds to be made.

One particular woman was very sick with the flu, had pneumonia on top of that, and was pregnant. She was so sick that she had to be given oxygen. The nun and I took turns watching her at night, and we ourselves got less and less sleep. She became worse. There were no airplanes coming to Fort George, and no way she could be sent to another hospital. I could see the nun doing her best to help her in every way she knew. Though I did not have much knowledge of medicine, even I could tell that she was beyond help. Some days she did not know us. We asked one of her relatives to come and stay with her, but he could not spare every day as he had children to mind. On top of all her discomforts, she ended up having a miscarriage.

The nun had asked me to watch the bed pan, and not to flush it down the toilet if I noticed anything. She wanted to examine it to make sure. She tried to describe to me what it would look like but I could not tell, no matter how I tried. I did not flush it down, but brought the pan to the nun each time. Finally, she noticed it and brought it to the dispensary. She put it in a little paper box, and explained to me that her religion did not allow her to discard it, no matter how small it was. I accepted her explanation; her sincere obedience to her religion impressed me greatly.

It had been a very trying day for me. My feet were aching and I felt so tired, but I never complained and neither did the nun. That same evening, the very sick woman died. It was late, and all the other patients were asleep. The nun spoke, "Here is where you have to control your nerves, and have confidence in yourself. Of all the things you have to do to be a nurse, this is the most difficult part for your mind, but you have to get over it and be strong. You will wash the dead body now, and I will show you where to begin." As I began to wash, my imagination went wild. Creeps were moving all over my body as I lifted her arms and legs to wash them. It was such an odd feeling, to move parts of her body and receive no response. I have kissed many dead bodies before they were buried, as my tradition demands it, but I had never handled a dead body.

I finished washing and put a clean gown on the body. I could hear every little noise, and my heart jumped each time. I could hear the nun cleaning the oxygen tent in another room. I went to her and told her that I was finished. She looked at me, searching into me, and I dared not show her how I felt, though I wanted to collapse in her lap. She was testing me, and again she asked me to go back to the room where the dead body lay, and bundle the woman's clothing so that the relatives could take them back first think in the morning. Creeps that I had thought were over came back again. I began to bundle up the clothing on a chair next to the white-sheeted body. I tried to convince myself that dead bodies do not revive like the stories I had heard from other children, that this dead woman was too nice and patient and had too kind a face to do such a thing. My mind was hurrying while my body tried to stay calm.

I went back to the nun, who had just finished. She looked tired, her rosy cheeks were pale, but she did not complain. She squeezed my shoulder with a gesture of appreciation and said with a shivering voice, "You are tired, tomorrow you can sleep as long as you want. I will tell the supervisor that you can miss chapel." I left and went up the stairs quietly to the third floor. All my roommates were sound asleep. I lay down and felt so tired, so tired that I could not think anymore and fell asleep with my clothes on.

I was up at noon, in time to have lunch, and went back to the hospital. The body had been removed, the relatives having taken it to the Anglican side to be buried. That same afternoon the nun and I went to bury the little paper box. She performed the rituals as her religion demanded.

Many of the patients improved and went home until we had just four patients again. Our work returned to normal. The mischievous boy was kept tied in his room with a baby harness and loosened everyday for a couple of hours to run around. He would let loose all over the place and run up and down the hall. We could hear him going everywhere. One day we heard him crying, coughing, and making vomiting sounds. The nun and I ran out to the hall and down to his room. Out he came, swaying like a little drunkard. We both ran to him. He smelled like the Lysol that we used to clean the toilets. There was a bottle of this in every bathroom. The nun brought him into the kitchen, and pushed her hands into his mouth. He began to vomit, and she kept forcing down some water and got him to vomit more. I checked his room while she worked on him. I could see that the harness string that had been tied to the legs of the bed had snapped. In the bathroom there was Lysol all over the floor, and its strong smell hung in the air. He could not have drunk too much, as the bottle was too heavy for him to hold to his mouth very long. Most of it had spilt on the floor. I cleaned up the room. I could hear the nun talking to him in French. She lectured him never to do that again. As for the nun and I, it was something extra on our hands, to check on him constantly, especially when he seemed too quiet. Though I felt weak each time these little catastrophes happened, somehow the sick gave me emotional strength.

What I Needed was Physical Strength

I was so tired that I was not feeding myself well, and in the mornings it was hard for me to get up. If I had not felt responsible to the nun and to my duties, I could have slept for a year. I did not complain, but she always knew how I was. She put me on vitamins; they perked my appetite, but my body wanted sleep. When the patients were many, she wanted me to wear a mask whenever I was near them. I hated that mask; my face would sweat, and I would feel as if I were suffocating. I could not stand it. When I knew the nun was not around, I would not bother to wear the mask, but only wore it when she was near. I was not getting over my fatigue, even though our routines were back to normal. The spring was coming, summer would follow, and I would go home. I felt elated to think that I would have a good rest at home where things were familiar. Yes, grandmother would take away my tiredness once I got home. I would be able to sleep all I wanted. I would hear birds singing all around our tent. When I went out and looked at the world, I would see seagulls hovering over our fish nets. Yes, everything would be fine once I got home again.

During this time the nun decided to take an X-ray of me. She examined it, but said nothing. In the evening, when our work was over, she showed me the X-ray, comparing it to the film that she had taken at the beginning of the year. There was a small spot on my left lung. She said it was vague, and she would have to send the X-ray to Moosonee Hospital to make sure. She sent the film on the first plane that spring. I think she had known all the time that something was wrong. She was so gentle when she told me — maybe it was nothing, that I should not exert myself anymore until we heard. I was put to bed. She let every girl from the school come to see me; all the nuns, priests, and brothers came to visit, a different one everyday. The first few days in bed were so welcome that it did not really bother me. All I wanted to do was sleep and sleep. I woke only for meals and wash times.

My want of sleep began to diminish, and I was restless in bed. I wanted to get up and around on my feet, and most of all, to go outside and smell the nice air. The nun came in to bring my food tray, to change my bed, and to make sure I got washed. She always had something to say to cheer me up. I guess she could see my anxieties. She began to keep my hands busy; once again, I wrote out labels for medicine bottles. It seemed I had done this before, so long ago.

Then came the news that the airplane was arriving from Moosonee. It was to stay overnight. The nun told me that I would have to go to Moosonee Hospital or to Moose Factory, she gave me a choice. She said that I had to take the proper tests and could only do so at either of these places. Early next morning all of the nuns, priests, and brothers came to say good-bye. I had not walked for a long time and I became tired in that short distance. I kept falling behind the two nuns who were to accompany me, yet they were walking at a normal speed. They, too, were going back to Moosonee, as they were due to be replaced by others.

We boarded the little plane which sat in the water, anchored to a little wooden pier. The pilot was different, but the plane was the same one that I had gone home on to Old Factory long ago. The plane took off, splashing water behind it. The engine was noisy to my ears. There were just the three of us and the pilot. We sat on little seats against the walls of the plane, no seat belts, and we felt every turn the plane made. It also carried cargo and mail. We were pioneers indeed, in the early flying days at Hudson and James bays.

We landed at Moose Factory. I had chosen to go to Moosonee Hospital as I felt that I knew the nuns there. Also, I had heard so many stories about the new hospital in Moose Factory — that they did not allow you to speak your own language, that the doctors pushed wires into your mouth and nose, that you had to be examined naked inside out, that they gathered your sputum and your urine in bottles.

The nuns made arrangements for us to be taken across to Moosonee by canoe. We took the same route that grandfather Symma had followed in taking me to the school when I was only five years old. That trip flashed through my mind as I wondered what would happen to me now. We arrived at Moosonee and walked up to the convent, the same building my grandfather Symma had taken me to when my face was covered with impetigo. At the door, the nuns were bubbling with happiness to each other. I stood beside them, feeling very lonely. One of the nurses came down and brought me to a room with two beds in it. She spoke to me with her arms, pointing at everything and speaking in French. I could see that she was not sure if I understood her or not. I did what she told me to do. I took a bath, changed to a gown, and bundled my clothing. I climbed into bed and cried silently. I thought about my parents, how I had flown over Old Factory that very day.

I had nothing to do; all I did was wash and have meals. Rarely did anyone come into my room, and my door was always kept closed. I was not examined. I was not given any medicine. I began to wonder what was wrong with me, and I would assure myself that I did not feel sick at all. The nuns were strange and cold, not like the ones at Fort George who had been so warm and helpful.

It was now July. A whole month had passed since I had come here. One evening there was a knock at the main door. I heard the swish of a long gown and the door opening. I could hear the nun speaking in Cree, and a few minutes later my father came into my room. What could I do? I cried and cried. I was so glad to see him. He had heard that I was in the hospital and had taken the navigating job again so that he could visit me. I wanted to tell him so much, but I had no words. I sat there on the bed while he gave me love sounds and advice: "Don't feel sad, don't disobey, don't think about home, you will only make yourself worse. Just listen to the doctors, and you will get better faster." He came once more and the next day left to return to Old Factory. I felt a little better, knowing that everybody was alright at home.

An Indian cleaning woman started to talk to me while she worked in my room. I began to look forward to seeing her. She asked what was wrong with me, and I replied that I did not know. Then she told me that a doctor from Moose Factory came over every month, that the nuns were probably just waiting for him. Sure enough, one day I heard a man greeting one of the nuns at the door. It was the doctor. Hopes and fears began to mix in my mind. Perhaps I would go home after he had seen me, or maybe there was something drastically wrong with me, maybe he would put wires down my throat. The doctor entered my room. I was neither glad nor frightened to see him. He greeted me in English and sat on my bed. His first question was, "Why didn't you come to Moose Factory Hospital?" I said I didn't know. "Did the nuns tell you not to go over there?" No. He told me that he could not find out what was wrong with me unless I went to Moose Factory, that all the necessary equipment was over there, and that if I went I would be with other Inuit people. He asked me if I would like that, and of course I said yes. He never examined me, didn't even take my pulse. It seems he had come only to convince me to move to Moose Factory, and he left just as suddenly as he arrived.

In a few days I was transferred over and put in a room with four empty beds. I was confined to bed, though I had to get up to wash and use the toilet. I could hear and see other Inuit and Indians when they walked up and down the hall. Some came in and stood for a few minutes at the foot of my bed. I did not know any of them; they were from other communities, and none from Old Factory River or Cape Hope. Everyday I was examined by different doctors and asked the same questions. No, I had never been seriously ill, other than those attacks. Some came twice to have me repeat the story of my attacks. I could not understand why such a common thing like that was so strange to the doctors. They were all mystified, and one of them admitted to never having heard of it. I was X-rayed again, my sputum and urine were gathered. Though I was examined all over my body, I was not examined inside. I kept expecting it, that all kinds of tubes would be put inside me. It never happened. But I was getting the sleep which I craved. I felt that I needed more physical strength than ever before; it was bad enough that woodpeckers were picking my brain.

We Were Shipped like Cargo

Within a few days, some of the patients who were up and around came into my room. They told me that there was an airplane leaving for *Inuitnnunanganut*, Inuit Land. The next day we could hear the plane leaving, that same evening the plane came back. Anyone who was allowed to be up ran to the windows and stuck out her head. Even the window of the room I was in was packed – heads, rear ends, and bare feet were all I could see from my bed, They were all trying to see if they could spot passengers as the plane landed on the river in front of the hospital.

They announced that they could see Inuit people as it flew by. Everybody wondered and hoped that it was not their husbands or their children. They all became silent, waiting for the next news. It was as though we were waiting for a thunderclap. Suddenly the silence was broken. I could hear a voice that was familiar, talking at the top of her lungs, announcing that she, too, had come to play in bed, followed by her well-known laugh. I would know that voice anywhere; it was my outspoken aunt. A group of women came into my room, already bathed, and in white gowns. They made a full stop when they saw me, even an Indian woman who was with them just stood there. In a few moments the three empty beds were filled. Nobody spoke, and I began to cry. They sat on their beds, and all three began to sooth me, and they told me that they did not want to see any more tears as they had had enough when they were leaving home. My outspoken aunt pleaded with me not to cry.

This was the woman who was to be my future mother-in-law. She told me the news from home, a bit here and there, that my parents had heard that I went far away, meaning south. "And here you are," she said, "it just shows that you cannot believe one word *qallunaat* say." She questioned, commented, teased, advised, and humoured everyone who came into the room. We never knew what she was going to say next. She made us laugh. She made us see the funny side of our situation, sometimes more or less convincing herself. Then she would become sad and think out loud, wondering how her children were, her husband, were they eating right? Did they have *kamiit* for the coming winter?

Now that I had seen the inside of a hospital and had nursed patients at Fort George, I was given a chance to view hospital life from the other side. Our days would start with breakfast, with washing and brushing our teeth. The ones that were up and able to go to the bathroom washed there. The others who were confined to their beds had to roll over to each side of the bed to allow the nurses to make them. I was in that situation. Every week we had different faces catering to us. The doctors and nurses were all imported from the south. The ward I was in became very fond of one particular nurse, and so did I. She had such a gentle face and nature. She tended to us without ever appearing impatient, her work was in her heart. She handed us our basins without throwing them at us. She had a way to human hearts, and we responded to her. When she was on duty, we behaved for her, her pleasantness kept us pleasant. When she was off duty, we were just the opposite. We wore long faces like the ones that were on duty. We sneaked around behind their backs. We ran to the windows to look out. They treated us like children, so we acted like children.

The weekly arrival of the train in Moosonee was exciting and saddening at the hospital. Patients looked forward to it because other patients would arrive back from the Hamilton Sanitarium on their way home, but it was also saddening, because someone would leave. The doctors would bring with them a translator and tell the patient that he or she had to go south to Hamilton. No preparation, no warning, no choice, and no reason given why they had to go so far away to be cured. One afternoon we boarded the train to Hamilton.

There were seven of us — two aunts, two men from Fort George, an Indian, a husband and wife from Great Whale River, and myself. My outspoken aunt never stopped talking, at times with humour, at times with sadness. Often she spoke to herself saying, "My little family is just getting further and further away. Will I ever see them again?" The rest of us kept quiet. We knew in our hearts that she spoke for all of us. She brought our feelings out into the open. All the way to Hamilton, I translated for them when our escort wanted to say something.

We arrived at Hamilton early in the evening and were met by the head nurse. We were put into an ambulance and driven to the hospital. For the next few days, all I did was translate for all kinds of nurses and doctors, back and forth between the rooms. The other four women were put next-door; in my room were all *qallunaat*. I did not see the men we travelled with since we were separated at the door. It seemed I never got to bed, translating all the time. I was beginning to think that there was nothing wrong with me. But I went through the whole examination again and was getting used to it by this time. Every time a different doctor came, I wondered if I would be told what was wrong with me at last. I translated for all the Inuit and Indians that I had arrived with. All were told what was wrong with them, what kind of medicine they were taking, and how long they could expect to be there. Me? I waited.

My *qallunaat* roommates began to urge me to ask when I would get needles like everybody else, to find out what was wrong with me. It is your body, they would say, and you have a right to know. The cultural beliefs that I was raised with and their urgings began to get mixed in my mind. My culture told me not to ask, that in this situation I might cause the people who were taking care of me to alter their behaviour completely, that I should accept what was happening and not force the hands that held my destiny. I figured that they would tell me when they were ready. I was X-rayed again, blood samples were taken, and the questions asked once more. Did I have such a complicated sickness that they did not know what to do with me? Finally, I was told that I had a spot on my left lung. I had known that at Fort George. It was not serious, but it was enough to put me to bed. I began to get needles. I dreaded them. Some nurses did not hurt, but others gave needles that sent pain all the way down my leg. We began to recognize which ones were not painful and which ones were. We called the days on which we were given needles "shot days." On shot days, we would wonder which nurse was coming. If it was one that we knew who pained, we all said, oh, no!

I asked one day if I could be up and around more, since I had to be up all the time to translate in the different rooms. The answer was no, I could not, as I might cause my lung to worsen. I could not understand that, why I would get worse if I walked a little more and strained my brain a little more when I translated. Yes, we were shipped like cargo and meant to behave like cargo.

We Kept Our Homes at the Backs of our Minds

A couple of months after our arrival, we were all moved to another building. We were put in one big room. There were eight of us, my two aunts, five *qallunaat* women, and myself. We all got to know each other. The *qallunaat* women were always visited by their relatives, and these, too, we got to know. They always brought fruit which was shared with us. Our only visitors were Red Cross people, and they were always in a hurry. They dropped us cigarettes and were gone as fast as they came in. I did not smoke, so I gave the packages to my aunts.

Time passed by until the month of December arrived. Everybody was talking about Christmas while my aunts talked about the cold weather at home, wondering how their families were, and how they were coping with their clothes for the winter. Some nurse would come in and tease my outspoken aunt about the cold weather outside, and she would laugh and say no, her face running with sweat. She would try to explain how much colder it was at her home. Arms in gestures of explaining would wave in every direction, and eventually I would rescue her by translating. The nurses could not believe what we told them about our winter weather. They could not believe that we could survive in such temperatures. They could not imagine that we had ways of keeping warm.

A week before Christmas I had two visitors, a man and his

wife. I had never seen them before. It was such a surprise to me that I cannot remember their names to this day. I know that they had kindly faces. They brought me a Christmas stocking, about three feet tall, all made of wire. It was stuffed with fruit, candy, and a pair of pyjamas. I did not know what to do or say. They spoke to me, but no words came out of my mouth. My mind was racing with thoughts. Who are these people? Why do they want to give me something like this? Was I a charity because I was in bed? The big wire sock sat at the foot of my bed. I kept looking at it. Everybody wanted me to open it up. The couple stood there while I felt awkward. They finally left, and all my roommates began to speak at once, some urging me to open it, some wondering who they were, some wondering why me? I wondered if they had made a mistake. I looked at the card that was tied to the sock, but it was no mistake. My name was written on it with all the Christmas wishes from the couple. I shared out the contents to all my roommates, and gradually the sock emptied. I could not store the sock anywhere to keep. It was taken out and probably put in the garbage. I kept looking out for the couple, and so did my roommates. They never came back.

Christmas came and went. I was knitting a lot, while my aunts were kept busy making Inuit dolls and parkas. Sometimes I stuffed the dolls for one of my aunts. Most of the time I was bored, and wondered what I could really do. Teachers came around, each trying to find out who would like to take up something. But permission had to be granted by the doctors if a patient wanted to take on an extra project. I got my permission, and took grade nine and ten in math, spelling and history. Now I was busy, ready to please my teacher who came around every week to see my work. All of us were doing something, one was taking art lessons, one was knitting, one who was from Yugoslavia took English.

The winter of 1952 passed by. To me it seemed that it had never come. I did not see much snow out the windows. Then summer came, and it was so hot! One of my aunts would suddenly throw down a parka she was sewing, "Whoever heard of making parkas in the summer?" She was so hot, and her face was constantly sweating. Even the fan on the ceiling did not do much good. In the midst of my complaints about the heat, my shots were stopped, and I began to be taken outside to walk on the lawn, as were my aunts. All three of us got excited, as we took it as a sign that we would soon be going home. My outspoken aunt kissed the grass, turning round and round, her arms outstretched. We could hear our roommates laughing from the windows with deep understanding. I sat there on the grass, looking at her and thought: how has she managed to be cooped-up indoors without going insane, when she was brought up out-of-doors? I was glad to be out, but even more so for her. What she was doing on the lawn, she was doing for all of us. No doubt she, too, had thoughts about home at the back of her mind.

Nightingale Kept Calling Me

One day I was called to the doctor's office. I was going home! There could be no other reason why the doctor would want to see me. I went down to the office where I usually translated for the doctors. Heads popped out of the rooms as I passed by them. One qallunaaq man whistled with his fingers between his lips. I felt insulted, as we whistle only to birds when we try to lure them while hunting. I ignored him and went on to the office.

I entered. The doctor was sitting at his desk. He offered me a chair and asked me how I was. He began, "You could help so much here. There will be more patients from your home. We could arrange for you to take up nursing, you could live at the nurses' residence, and if you don't like it, you could always go home." Just like that! "Thank you," he said, and I left.

I sat on my bed thinking, thinking, thinking. On my way to the office I had been so excited, now I was all mixed up. My roommates were asking about the meeting. There was a nurse in the room making beds, and she explained it to them all. Apparently she already knew the course of my future. In the midst of my thoughts I heard her say, "Yes, she is certainly needed by her people here." I thought no more. I knew that there were not many Inuit who spoke English at that time. I could not stand the idea of them coming here, given this and that without understanding. I thought, too, that people have a way to make one feel guilty when they want and need you. I would feel guilty if I left all these Inuit and Indians. Those at home had done without me this long; they were only waiting for me to get married. I was not prepared for that yet.

So I moved into the nurses' residence within the following few days. Here was something new I had to get used to again. I had my own room. All together I was on my own, there was nobody there to get me up, to bring my breakfast, to turn out the lights or to tell me when to take a bath. Though the surroundings were the same, as were the faces, the change was tiring. I could tell that I had not used my body for a long time. I was put to work in the children's ward. There I was given my instructions by the head nurse. Once a week I spent time with another nurse, reading anatomy books. She would have me memorize all of the body names. Each week she gave me a chapter to work on. Fortunately I had been taught by my people to memorize, a skill that has been practised by my people for generations, be it story-telling or travel routes. My supervisor would be so mad that I did not take notes. When we were learning all those Latin words, she would be amazed how I knew them by heart. She would say that I was careless because I did not make notes. She did not see that I compiled everything in my head. I never tried to explain to her how I knew the answers and she never bothered to ask. Sometimes, without warning, my supervisor at the children's ward would get a phone call — someone needed me to translate in another building. I might be in the middle of my lessons, but would drop everything and go. This would happen on my days off as well.

I was enjoying my adventure, though my home was always at the back of my mind. I kept telling myself that I could go home at any time. My two aunts had gone back by then. I would think about them, how close they were to the sea. Here at the hospital, all I saw were trees, tall buildings, cars, and many lights at night. I had no special friend, no one I could talk to about my thoughts. As far as I was concerned, I was there only temporarily and did not

179

try to make friends. The nurses and doctors spoke to me only when they needed a translator. Otherwise I was different and strange to them. The people I worked with were polite, that was all. They didn't stand around with me to discuss little personal experiences, as they did among themselves.

I saw and I heard. I never made known my feelings or frustrations. Though I was enjoying this adventure and found my classes challenging, there was something missing. Humanity was not there, that which I had been brought up to need. I missed it, but I also learned how to ignore it when it wasn't there. I kept telling myself that I would know and feel it again once I got home.

Home was just Meant to be a Memory

Two years went by, and I received a letter from my father saying that I had a duty to come home, that my aunt had told him that I was not needed where I was, that there were a lot of nurses. Whatever she told him, he wanted me home right away. My aunt knew him well; by telling him that there were plenty of nurses here, he would soon have me home so that I could marry her son.

I went to my head nurse and told her that my father wanted me home. She asked if there were any problems at home, or if it was an emergency. Or did I want to go home that badly? I said yes. I could not be bothered to explain to her that there were certain things arranged in my culture. I don't think she would have understood. She took a deep breath and said, "You have one year before you finish nursing, that is not long before you are certified." I just sat there, not answering, even though my head was saying stay and finish, and my heart was saying go home and stop worrying your father. I longed for home. She spoke again, "A year is not a loss, you can go home and come back and finish. I will make all the arrangements." I left to pack.

My mind wanted to stay, but my heart was singing with joy. The head nurse advised me not to pack all my things, but to leave some of them behind; I could always send for them if I did not come back. She drove me down to the train station early in the morning. I sat in the car, not saying anything, while she talked and talked, reminding me that I had much to give to my people. Though I could hear her clearly, her meanings were not sinking in. All I could picture were my home and my family. She gave me a hug and said goodbye. I boarded the train and sat close to the window. The train began to move. I sang in my heart, neither seeing nor hearing the other passengers.

Then it hit me that I was completely alone, on my own on a strange travel route. I had no one to speak to. I had to start thinking. I had to remember what the head nurse had said about changing trains, where to eat, who to ask for assistance. I began to find the trip long, and anxieties grew that I might take the wrong train while changing. Then I heard the conductor shout the name of the next stop, and I wondered if he would shout about the next change. He did – I could have jumped up and given him a hug, but I didn't. Instead I told myself that he was doing his duty well. The train changed at North Bay. I did not have to wait long, and again I sat near a window. I felt hungry and decided to go to the dining car. As I made my way through the train every head turned to stare at me. I stared back. Grandmother's voice came to my mind; she used to say that if I wanted to stare, I should at least stare with a pleasant smile. They didn't smile back, they just looked away.

While I was gone, a man had sat down next to my seat. He got up to give me room when I returned. He began to ask me what part of the Arctic I came from. It was amazing to meet a qallunaaq who knew right away what my nationality was. He had been a Hudson's Bay Company clerk for many years on Baffin Island, and now he was on his way to Moosonee and Moose Factory, travelling for Northern Affairs. Though I felt very shy, I was glad to talk to him. The next day we arrived at Moosonee. He looked after me with such protection; I felt for once that somebody was with me who understood Inuit minds, who knew that I was in a strange land. While I waited in Moosonee for the plane to Old Factory I showed him where I had gone to school. The building was no more, but a new one was standing not far from the old location, and it still bore the name St. Thomas Anglican School. We went down to where the Indian village had been; now it was all houses, no more tepees. I showed him the church to which all the school children had marched in long line-ups every Sunday, so long ago when I was only five years old. Though I did not tell him, I remembered, too, the time my grandfather and father had arrived to take me out of school. I looked at the river bank where I had boarded the little plane. I could recall the pillow case bag that was full of toys, that I had dropped in the water just as I was climbing up the steps. That was one thing that hadn't changed; the loading pier was still there. It looked so small now that I was older.

The next day I was boarding at the same pier, into the plane with two suitcases. I was the only passenger; the plane was full with mail and parcels. We skimmed along the water and my heart began to pound as the plane climbed higher and higher. It was such a beautiful day, not a cloud in the sky. Below us the water was deep blue. I kept looking out the window until I could recognize the landmarks. They looked small from the plane, but they were all familiar. We were circling Old Factory River. I could see houses and people moving around. I scanned over the area where Inuit people have always tented. There was only one tent. I could see a motor canoe racing towards the plane's landing spot. We touched the water, and the plane crawled slowly to its anchoring site. The engine stopped, and the motor canoe approached more slowly. I didn't recognize the man in the canoe. The pilot opened the door just as he anchored to the plane. It was my little brother – he had grown so much! He had a very shy smile. We just looked at each other for a few seconds. I wanted to hug my brother and lumps were in my throat. I was fighting my tears.

As we approached the Inuit dock area I could see that swarms of people had gathered. I felt shy. Among all those Indians my grandmother stood out clearly. She walked down to help steady the bow of the canoe. Oh, it was good to hear the sound of the canoe rubbing against the rocks. I jumped out of the canoe and gave grandmother a hug. I wanted to hold her there for a long time, but I was aware of the audience behind her. As I climbed up to the bank, each of our Indian friends came over to shake my hand; all said something to help the happy event. Grandmother and I walked up to our tent while brother put away the canoe. As we walked the path that the Inuit have walked for many years, I became aware of nature around me. Bees were buzzing, butterflies flying, birds singing, and mosquitoes trying to bite. The seagulls that used to hover over the fish nets were still there, diving up and down. It was a clear, beautiful day. We entered two tents that stood facing each other. Grandmother lived on one side and father on the other. It was so good to be in the tent again and to feel the fresh air all around.

Grandmother began to tell me the news; first, father had been to Moose Factory Hospital with a broken finger. He came back and then left again to navigate the same boat he had been handling for many years. Just grandmother and brother were there at Old Factory; they had come for my arrival. The rest of the Inuit were all at Cape Hope. Brother had grown so much, both physically and mentally. We didn't tease each other anymore. He showed me his sleeping area. He now had his own covers, and his own separate spot. He was proud of that because it was a sign of growing up. We had fresh netted fish for supper, and all three of us went to bed early.

Grandmother had not changed her ways; after serving me breakfast in bed for a couple of days, she began to tell me to go out and look at the world. Brother and I fell into our routine chores. Somehow they were not the same anymore as we were not fighting. I did not miss the fighting; everything seemed to be done much faster. We had a lot of idle time. But grandmother always found something for us to do. The arrival of the ships was still an event, but all the other Inuit were not there to enjoy it. The RCMP ship arrived, and as always we were asked to produce the disks which carried our numbers. They asked who had given birth and who had died, and then they left.

A few weeks went by. Though I could tell that grandmother was happy to have me home again, she acted strange a lot of the time. It was as though she was nervous about something. I could feel that she wanted to discuss some matter with me, but she never really came out with it, whatever it was. One morning when we awoke, the weather was terrible, and the sea was raging. Grandmother said that there must be a ship nearby, coming to Old Factory. Her belief was that the crew of the ship was shaving, that the sea did not like the hairs — it caused the sea to itch and made it rage.

During this wind and rain, I went out to look at the world. I stood for a second, and there in the raging sea I saw a canoe with two people in it. Their canoe was appearing and disappearing in and out of the waves. I ran back into our tent and told grandmother. She watched for awhile and said that there must be bad news from Cape Hope Island. She could tell by the way the two men were arriving, their motor cut off, as that is a sign which we use to prepare the people on land for bad news.

They docked their canoe beside ours in front of our tent. They came in, very sad. It was Weetaltuk's youngest son, Pili, and my *angilissiak*. Grandfather Weetaltuk had died; he had not been sick, nor did he ever say that he was sick, but he was found dead in his bed. He had been our faithful leader for fifty years. He always got us through hard times; we never went hungry as he always had an instinct for knowing where the animals would be in certain seasons. I wondered what would happen now to the Cape Hope Islanders. Would they choose another leader or just drift apart? Or would the government move them to another settlement? (The government wasted no time and moved them to Great Whale River. There the group was no more. Such a proud people just mingled in with the other crowds who had to rely on an alien culture for survival.)

I had no tears even though my heart was heavy. I did not accept his death right away. I kept telling myself that strong and towering men don't die and leave their duties. Had I been to his death rituals and participated in his funeral, I would have accepted it more easily. Even though I know that the Cape Hope Inuit are no longer there, I still think Weetaltuk lives on.

I became aware of our company who were having hot tea and fresh fish. They were talking to grandmother and asking where my father was. Pili, who is my *sanarik*, my builder, commented on how I had grown into a woman. He looked proud, as he had had a lot to do with the shaping of my mind. My *angilissiak* sipped his tea and smiled. He was the one who had been waiting for me to grow up, according to the arrangements made the day I was born. He was my future husband. I began to wonder why these two particular men, who had had a lot to do with my birth, had been sent to notify us. No doubt both of them had been sent to discuss my marriage. Grandmother said little, as did the men. They probably felt awkward, especially since my father was not there. He would have consented right there and then.

I felt nothing. As far as I was concerned, I was in the hands of the people who knew the course of my future. I could not fight my elders, but nothing was said. I looked at my brother, and for the first time since I arrived, he had a teasing look on his face. He did not have to speak. I could see what he was thinking, "Ho, ho, my sister is going to be married off." He thought it was funny because both of us knew nothing of what marriage was all about. We were both scared, intrigued, and had accepted the fact that that was what people eventually did when they had grown. But nothing happened.

The two men left after a couple of days' trading and after notifying the *qallunaat* authorities of the death. The three of us stayed put and waited for father. Grandmother's nerves seemed to be on edge. I could tell she had a lot on her mind. She had been this way since my arrival, but I did not dare ask her anything. In a few days we heard that the big Hudson's Bay ship was on its way. I guessed they were the ones who were shaving their beards, who made the sea rage. In the evening, while brother was out checking our nets, grandmother spoke nervously. "Minnie, you will never survive with that man. He is too lazy, he will bring nothing from his hunting trips. I have taught you well, not for a lazy man. You will go away and go back to school when the ship arrives." My mind was confused and feelings were jumbled up, full of question marks. She must be right, she is my elder, I have no way to answer her. But surely she is not serious to send me away. What about my father? He is not even here, I haven't seen him yet, where will I go? As always, she could see the questions in my mind. "You will stay with your cousin Nellie who is at Moose Factory." I did not know the cousin grandmother was talking about. She was originally from Fort George, and at one time it was thought she might be my future step-mother, but I had never met her. She was married now to a boy who had emigrated from Belcher Islands to Cape Hope. I hardly knew her, even though she was in some way related to grandmother; him, I knew as a rabble-rouser in our community.

I could see that grandmother had no choice, nor had I. I had always thought that she would be the one who would force me to marry and follow the traditions, but it was not so. Grandmother was anxious for me to leave before father returned. My thoughts returned to Moose Factory; it seemed I had just come from there. I came to grips with myself and planned to go back to Hamilton and finish nursing. Then it occurred to me that I had no money for either transportation or food, let alone for accommodation. I did not have a penny. I could not tell grandmother about my private worries, she would not understand. She thought that everybody was like the Cape Hope Islanders, who helped you out when in need. Grandmother was determined that I leave and encouraged me to pack.

The ship arrived from Fort George on its way back to Moose Factory. The three of us walked down to our docking area, and there I said goodbye to grandmother. Brother took me over to the ship. I felt too embarrassed to ask right out if I could have a free ride. The captain looked so enormous, standing there on the deck. He helped me up and told me to get inside if I were cold. I just stood there, not moving, and watched brother turning back. We had not said a word to each other and spoke only with gestures of sadness. I kept thinking about my father, that I had not even seen him when he was the one who had written such an urgent letter, telling me that I had a duty to come home. It was in the middle of the morning, and the ship was moving slowly out the Old Factory River fiord. I stood on the same spot and looked at the scene that I have gazed on so often. The landmarks seemed to say look at us a little longer, you will remember us well.

After breakfast the next morning I was put ashore at Moosonee and caught a ride over to Moose Factory with an old Indian friend from Fort George. He knew my father well. I asked him where my cousin was living, and he pointed to an area at the edge of the trees, not far from the river bank. I gave him a thankful smile and walked up.

As I reached the sandy bank, I stopped. I looked to the right, there was the hospital and a row of houses just behind it. I looked to the left, where the man had pointed, and there were trees and a path. I found my cousin living in a small tent with nothing on her floor, just earth. I was used to tents that had wooden floors. She was sitting among blankets, sewing, and a small baby was sound asleep beside her. I told her who I was. She welcomed me happily. I could tell she was very lonely. Her husband was working now at the hospital. They were the only Inuit at Moose Factory, other than the ones in the hospital. The rest were all Indians and qallunaat.

Many things went through my mind. My cousin's parents would have been shocked if they could have seen her living like this. I knew she had been born and raised in a solid house. We spoke shyly to each other. She looked so tired and underfed. I had to think of a way to get out of there so she wouldn't have an extra worry with me. Her husband came home and broke my thoughts. I shook his hand and was glad to see him, and that was all. I had known him for many years, and I knew he had a bad temper. I cautioned myself to be very careful of how I behaved or what I said in front of him. I never knew what might trigger his temper, and I hoped to leave them as a friend at least.

I did not feel that way about her. She was gentle, kind, and understanding — the kind of woman all Inuit men dream about and want to keep safe and secure. She had nothing like that. Already that evening he was mad at her because his tea was not ready. She said nothing and went on to make the tea, more or less humouring him. He dropped his anger when he remembered my presence. We all went to bed with what few spare blankets they had. I was cold all night, but fell asleep with a last thought that I must find a job, or go back to school. The husband was leaving for work when I awoke. The baby was crying. She came running in and put the baby on her back with a shawl. I got up and dressed, went out, and looked at the world. At least the sky promised a nice day. I joined her at the fire, and both of us ate some oats. I told her about my plans and left shortly for the hospital and school.

I went to the school first and stood for a long time in a hall near an office. The principal finally came down the stairs. He asked me what I wanted and I told him. I could not go back to school there, the grades did not go beyond the eighth. He told me that I would have to go away to Sault Ste. Marie, or find a job. I left the school and walked back towards my cousin's tent, thinking about what I could do next.

When I arrived back at the tent, my cousin was washing diapers by hand, her baby on her back. I offered to take the baby while she finished. Later we sat outside and discussed my prospects. I did not want her to know that I felt it was hopeless, but she knew and could see. I could stay with her as long as I wanted, she said, though she felt that I did not deserve such a poor home. I tried to reassure her and gave her an understanding smile. Then she began to tell me about her marriage, how hard it was, that she had never thought she would experience such cruelty. She had a fear in her voice; she was amazed that anyone could have such a bad temper, sometimes over nothing. "However," she said, "I put myself here, the mistake is mine. I should have listened to my father and married your father. I was bothered by the difference in our ages and so married a young man who needs to be brought up a little more. I had nothing against your father but his age. Now that I have met you, I am sorry; your father must have a great deal of sense, to have a daughter with a nature like yours. I know that I should not think like this, to allow another man to enter my mind, but I have to say it. Maybe I will never have another chance to apologize." Then she gave a little laugh and said, "Look at me, I look old enough now from all this worry to be your mother."

She was making light of her situation, just what an Inuk would do, even though she had fear in her voice. We realized how late it was getting, and she quickly got up and lit the fire to make tea. Yes, I could see that she was trained to keep peace, just as other Inuit women are shown by example how to humour their men. Grandmother used to have a saying, don't let him spill. She thought of a man's temperament as a cup full of water; if you handle him without spilling, he is fine, but should you spill, watch out for his impatience.

Her husband came home from work. Surprisingly, he was in a happy mood, much joy to his wife. He left again shortly after to go down to the village. We women sat again and talked some more. She said that she had not experienced this kind of peace for a long time, that perhaps I was controlling his temper because he was ashamed to show it to me, that perhaps I could live with them. I sat and thought. I decided to be honest with her and told her that I planned to find a job and my own room, and to go home next summer when the ships were running again. She understood and did not blame me for how I felt. I told her that I wanted to go to the hospital early in the morning, and I went to bed. She, too, got under the blankets not long after I did. I was just falling asleep when her husband returned. He was noisy and loud with his mouth. In no time, the little tent was filled with the smell of liquor. He had been drinking. I was scared because I had heard that liquor made people lose their minds. I lay there, not moving, pretending to sleep. Eventually he became quiet, and I slept fitfully.

The hospital was the only place where I might find a job. (There was the Hudson's Bay Company, but they did not hire natives.) I went to see the administrator, who had no manners whatever and not one polite word. I could see that he felt very important with himself and was eager to impress the natives with his high and mighty job. He hated his job because there was no one there who understood his importance. He was not listening when I introduced myself, but I began, "I want an office job, I type forty words a minute and know how to file. I am also interested in nursing." With a show of impatience, he told me that the qallunaaq girl would give me a test in typing. I sat there while she prepared some papers. I was so determined to get a job that I lost all my nervousness.

Suddenly, the administrator appeared again. One of his secretaries had not come in; apparently she was having problems with her babysitter. His voice became loud. "Phone Mrs.

Qallunaaq So-and-So, and get her over here." He pointed to me. "Send her over to babysit." His manner reminded me of a child who was not getting his own way. He disappeared into his office. I could tell the girl was feeling awkward, she had to listen to him, and yet she tried to be polite to me.

I was taken to the woman's house by a girl from Moose Factory, an old schoolmate of mine. She told me that this woman had a different babysitter almost every week, and no wonder. The whole house was a mess, toys all over the floor and dishes piled up in the sink. My former schoolmate left. The woman's orders were to keep the house clean and to make sure the children were clean and taken care of. Did I cook? At that time I had never cooked any food other than fish, seal, whale, geese and ducks. Make bread? I couldn't even remember how to dissolve yeast as I had learned in home economics at school. She never gave me a chance to answer any of her questions, as she was one of those women who talk without stopping to listen to an answer. I was amazed that she was willing to hire me and leave her young children in my hands, when she didn't even wait for my answers. Obviously, she was desperate. She asked me to watch her children for the day, and she left to go back to work.

I suddenly felt a great responsibility fall on me. But I looked at it as a challenge and told myself that another job would come my way, that I wouldn't be there long. I became aware of the two little children sitting on a worn-out couch. They were making strange with me. I went over and sat on the couch next to them. I asked for their names and they told me. Both had English accents, just like their mother. I showed them that I was harmless and spoke to them at their level. Both began to bring out their toys to show me. The more I was interested in their toys, the more came out, until the whole area was full of toys. I could see that they were beginning to relax with me. I fell in love with them. I gave the four-year-old a hug, and immediately the two-year-old came forward. I hugged her, too. They became all the more confident and started running around, in and out the back door. I let them go on as long as they were not in danger. The four-year-old asked if we could go to the hospital confectionery to see his father who worked there. I said no firmly. They were testing me to find out how much I was willing to let them have their own way. I reminded them of the toys on the floor, the way I have been taught in my culture to distract children. Besides, I was not ready to meet the father. God knows what he was like!

The morning went by, and the mother came home for lunch. All four of us sat at the table and ate toast covered with beans. That was easy enough, I thought. The woman was less hurried by this time and began to ask me where I had come from. She appeared loving to her children, but I could tell that she had no time to express her affection all the time. She was a working woman. She was originally from England and had married during the last war. She explained to me how she had met her husband. I was not interested in her past life just then. All I wanted from her was understanding and patience until I knew what she expected of me, and that she would let me go home the next summer. She understood my predicament and told me that I could move in with her family that very night. She would pay me twenty dollars a month and I could have days off if I wanted. She would show me how to cook. I did not say anything, nor did I ask any questions, I just gave her gestures of understanding. Then her lunch hour was over, and she had to go back to work. She called out to her children goodbye, and they both replied cheerfully. She seemed surprised and asked me what I had done to them. She said that she had never been able to leave without them crying and pulling at her dress. She looked relieved and said, "They like you," then left for the hospital.

The afternoon passed by happily, the children contented to play outside. I sat on the steps and watched them both. I thought about my new situation and assured myself that I would find another job more suited to my dreams. For the moment, I had to accept what came my way and do it well. I had to enjoy it and learn from it as much as I could — such is the way of thinking that I had been taught by my people.

The woman returned late in the afternoon. She greeted me with a smile and asked if the children had been bad. To me, that was a strange question; in my culture, we expect children to be bad and good, and that parents will teach them the difference. I did not answer her, but only returned her cheerful smile. She had decided that I would stay for supper and meet her husband. I thanked her and stood watching while she peeled potatoes. She mentioned again that I could move in and have my own room. She wondered if I would like to do so that evening after supper. I was not answering as I was thinking about the whole idea, wondering what I was getting into. I wondered if she would let me go once I decided to leave for something else. She knew my situation well. She knew that there would be no ships or planes leaving for my home until next summer. She knew about the people I was staying with. She knew everything that went on outside her home; it was a small community.

The front door opened, and a towering, red-haired man entered. He went straight to the children and lifted them both in his arms. He put them down and tickled their tummies. He looked so happy to see them, and the children were delighted. The little boy asked if he knew Minnie. Minnie who, he asked, still funning. He looked surprised when he saw me and asked his wife who I was while he kissed her on the cheek. "This is Minnie, who is going to look after the children. Minnie is staying for supper." Minnie this and Minnie that. She told him everything she knew about me, that I might be moving in with them. He was quiet, standing there, looking at me and sizing me up. Finally, he asked me who my father was. He knew him and knew that he navigated ships in the summer.

During supper the children and I were quiet while they discussed their day at work. He was the manager at the confectionery. His father had been a settler from Scotland, and his mother was a native of Moose Factory. He looked like a Scottish whaler with a deep sense of humanity and the humour of an Indian. He was very outspoken and commented that I ate like a mouse. I ate even slower and smiled, my eyes glued to my plate. She asked him not to tease. He suddenly got up and practically ran into the kitchen. She followed him. Something was wrong; though I felt very shy, I could feel his doubts. He did not hide anything, not even his words. He began to throw questions at her. "How long is she going to last? How old is she? Fifteen? Sixteen? Does she know how to care for small children? Look at her, she is so slow! She wouldn't move if a bomb fell. Our children are picking up all kinds of things from these week-to-week babysitters!"

He spoke no more. She was calm and calming him at the same time. She knew how to placate him. She came over to me and more or less apologized for the outburst. I just smiled at her to let her know that I understood, but my own feelings were confused. She asked me not to mind what her husband said, that he was not all that mean. Once I got to know him, he would be like a father to me. I could see that she was determined to hire me. He came into the kitchen and spoke, "Christ, you women sure know how to make a man feel small and guilty." He banged the counter with his fist right in front of me and said, "You are hired! Come at nine o'clock tomorrow morning with your belongings."

The next morning I got up and arranged my two suitcases which had hardly been unpacked since I had arrived. I went out and looked at the world; it was the same as the day before, just beautiful. I told my cousin that I would come to see her when I was free and tried to thank her for her kindness. As I left, I turned around to look at her. She was standing and watching, her hands wiping tears from her eyes. I knew that she was not crying for me, because I was not going very far. She was crying because I had been able to give her some peace and had controlled her husband's temper. She lived in constant fear.

I walked on, and at my new home the woman opened the door and was so cheerful, talking a mile a minute. She had the bed all made in my room and the closet emptied. I had a bedside table and a chest of drawers. I put my two suitcases near the bed. She hurried on to get to work and left. The children were still in their pyjamas, toast crumble on their cheeks. They were cute and bubbling, and I gave them my full attention. Home was just meant to be a memory, and one makes the best one can of the present.

House Work is a Lonely Affair

A couple of months passed by. As she had promised, the woman showed me what to do everyday. Every morning, before she left for work, she would tell me how to prepare the roast, the pork chops, the hamburger, beans, bread, or whatever. Eventually I took over the meal plans and chores. Some I knew that I did well, and some I just could not, especially mashing potatoes. One day the husband called me into the kitchen while I was setting the table. "Stand right there and watch," he said. He began to mash the potatoes, adding to them salt, butter and milk. I had been putting in only salt. "That is how you mash potatoes," he said, slamming the masher on the counter. That is how I have mashed potatoes ever since. Each time I put down the masher, gently, I still hear the bang, loud in my memory. He was not angry or mean, he was just that kind of teacher.

That was the only complaint I heard from him. I did not receive any from her. She was just so glad that I was there while she was able to go out to work. She seemed lonely. She hardly had any company. Slowly, she began to tell me her worries, anxieties, and interests. She began to tell me who should be my friends and who should not. She told me about a woman down the street who gave piano lessons. She had spoken to her and made arrangements for me to go in the evenings, once a week, for fifty cents an hour. I began my lessons. The teacher was the wife of one of the doctors at the hospital. She, too, had an English accent. I was her only native student, the rest were all *qallunaat* children.

I had met and come to know many *qallunaat* by then and had learned to be cautious with them. Some were nice and kind, but none wanted to see or understand my native culture. Some didn't want to know, some didn't have time, some found it too deep to understand or accept. They all wanted to cover it up with their ways. They always wanted me to be different, a novelty, and they refused to see that I was a plain human being with feelings, aches, pain, joy, happiness, gratitude, and all the other things that every other being was capable of having. They thought that the Inuit were nothing but a bunch of smiling, happy people.

One evening I arrived at the teacher's house and as usual took off my coat and sat myself at the piano. She came into the room directly from the kitchen. She never had greeted me, ever; just gave me the lesson and showed me the pages of the books I was to follow. This evening she did not get on with the lesson, but spoke. "You natives are so talented, you natives should take advantage of your free education, you natives should aim for higher things." You natives should this and that. I just sat there taking it all in. She had never spoken so much to me before. I was not answering, though I was thinking that no one had ever shown us how to use our talents to their full capacity. No one had ever told us that we received a free education, or shown us what their way of education might prepare us for. Nobody had told us what was high or low in this culture we were forced to learn.

She gave me a page to follow on the piano and disappeared into the kitchen. I sat a few seconds and thought. I felt frustrated. I felt that she should show me how to use her way of education to full capacity, not condemn me with a slur against "natives." She forced it out like a dirty word. For the first time, I felt a hint of hate growing inside me; I did not have to take this stranger's attitudes in my land and home. I folded the page she had given me and with all my heart, played a tune I once performed at a school concert. I played it right to the end, loudly and with my fingers shaking. I rose, took my coat, and went out. I never went back again. I had learned long ago that you don't hang around when you are not really wanted.

My daily chores went on, day in and day out. I could do my tasks in no time, and the children were not the handful they had been at the beginning. But I felt very lonely. Nobody visited me, my old schoolmates did not want to come. They felt alright with the man of the house — some of them were related to him — but they felt strange with her. A few said that she was too stiff and cold. I did not find her that way, or perhaps I was just used to her. Instead, I visited them, but all were doing something, some working, some married, and some going steady with boyfriends. They had no time for me. My cousin had moved into her new house, and I went to visit her one evening. I was pained when I saw her condition. She had a black eye, and one side of her face was all colours, pink, blue, red and black. I did not have to ask her what had happened. She began to cry and blurted out all her fears. She begged me to move in with her. I gave her gestures of sympathy and told her that I would speak to the woman I worked for. I went back home, and everybody was in bed. My cousin's bruised face kept coming to my mind before I fell asleep.

The next day I spoke to the woman and told her that I wanted to move in with my cousin, that I would come everyday at nine o'clock. She looked shocked and said that she would discuss it with her husband that evening. He would not hear of it. "Do you know the people?" he asked. I nodded yes with my head. "Christ, he beats his wife, imagine what he would do to you. No! You are in our hands, you are under our care. We would feel responsible if harm should come to you." As usual he got up and stomped to the kitchen, as he always did when he was lecturing. He came back to the table and continued, "You are welcome here, we have taken you in as part of our family. You eat well, you have a private room. Do you know that this is the first time the children have had anyone they liked? Over there, you won't even get your sleep, you will be up all night while he's drinking, and he might even get you to drink. You go and tell that cousin of yours that you can't move in with her."

I went the next day and told my cousin that I did not want to move in. I never mentioned what the man had said; I did not have to, as she understood. But I still visited her once in awhile. She always had a lot to say about her feelings and needed to get rid of her bottled-up emotions. I gave her no advice, nor did I make her any promises. She had another baby girl and died a few years later. She was so young. Whatever killed her probably had much to do with her living conditions. Her husband has since married again. He drinks, but does not get drunk anymore. He has started a new family. I guess he is one of those people who learn slowly, and become wise in later years, at a terrible cost to others.

Gradually, the woman had me doing the grocery shopping down at the Hudson's Bay. She asked me to shop for the children's clothes. Sometimes I felt that the children were my own. They cried to me, they expressed their fears and joys to me, they called for my help, they ran to me when they were in pain and asked me to kiss away their aches. I was in their parents' hands, but the house and the children were in mine. Though I loved the two children, my whole self craved for company with whom I could talk at my level. Physically I was very busy, but spiritually I was empty. I learned that house work is a very lonely affair.

I Still Knew How to be Happy

Winter came, and sometimes I would go to hockey games. A team would come over from Moosonee and play with the hospital team. Christmas came and passed. Then spring was in the air. Thoughts of home preoccupied me. I began to take longer walks with the children. They enjoyed the fresh air as much as I did.

One day, during one of my usual walks, I met up with the Moose Factory Indian agent. He always said hello when I saw him, but today he stopped me and said, "Minnie, have I got good news for you! You are wanted in Ottawa, you have a job there." Normally he did not have a serious nature, so I did not believe him. Who knew me in Ottawa? I walked off and told him that he was teasing. He yelled back that he was serious. "Come and see me in my office sometime, when you get the time," he said. I did not answer him again and altogether forgot the whole episode.

I began to wonder how I should approach the couple about wanting to go home. I knew the ships would be running soon, but I kept putting it off as I did not know how to go about it. Though I longed for my own people, I felt happy and accepted by the couple, especially by the children. Time went by, and the news was in the air that the ships were running. I still didn't know how to approach the couple. The longer I left it, the harder it became for me to tell them that I wanted to leave. They had no idea, of course, I had never mentioned the subject of home to them. They acted as though I was there permanently. She made plans for all of us to have a summer holiday, and I said nothing. Who was I to shatter her dreams?

One day they came home early, both full of excitement. He spoke first. "Minnie, have you got a surprise coming! You had better change!" The wife told me not to wash the dishes that night. They wouldn't tell me what it was all about. I felt a little scared, because I thought they might be trying to fix me up with a boyfriend. They had mentioned several times that I should find one. I changed while they made supper. We ate, and they did the dishes, all the while watching the clock which hung over the sink in the kitchen. The children were put to bed, and then the three of us sat in the living room.

Suddenly there was a knock at the front door; the man ran to answer it, and she got up, too. Two men came in, one was a tall Indian, and the other was short, tanned, and ugly as ever. It was my father! I jumped off the couch, and went to him. He gave me a grown-up caress. I shook hands with his partner, and we all sat down. I wanted to say so much to my father. I wanted to tell him that I longed to go home. I hoped he would order me to go home in front of the couple. But nothing came out of my mouth; we both felt too awkward to speak our language in front of these people who did not understand us. That was something we did not do, unless it was an ugly situation. So, he began to talk to the man. The Indian sat there and listened. I had never heard the man speak his mother's tongue before, but he conversed easily with my father in Cree. They talked about ships, Old Factory, and hunting.

The woman made coffee and served everyone. She looked uncomfortable, still very English in her ways after having been among her husband's native people all these years. Somehow I couldn't ignore her, it was as though I was seeing her for the first time. I often wondered why his relatives did not visit, not even his parents who came to see their grandchildren only at Christmas. I imagined that the parents had picked out a wife for him while he was away during the war in England. Instead, he had come home with one who was a stranger to his own people. Perhaps the parents had accepted and welcomed her, but could not melt that cold middle-class English nature. Perhaps she was shocked by the wilds of Canada. Who knows? It could have been anything. However, I saw her for the first time that evening, and somehow I could not help but feel sorry for her.

Father and his partner visited for a couple of hours more and then left to return to the ship at Moosonee. He said he would come back the next day. The three of us sat for awhile. The man began to tease me. "How can such an ugly father produce such a pretty girl? I could not believe that he was your father when he was brought to the confectionery this afternoon!" Then she spoke, first to him. "Do you always have to be so outspoken? You are insulting Minnie!" She did not have to worry about that. I had always known that father was not the best-looking, but he had a heart as big as all outdoors, kind and loving. She continued, "He must care an awful lot for you. How many fathers would come all the way from Old Factory to see their daughters? Do you think he will ask you to go home? Surely, you don't want to go home?" Of course, she did not wait for my answer, but she was thinking and so was her husband. Then he began, "Christ, you wouldn't go just like that would you? You don't even have time to pack. We couldn't replace you in one day. It would take weeks for us to find someone else. I'll speak to him myself tomorrow." That was the end. We all went to bed before I had a chance to speak for myself. I lay in bed thinking, and realized that it was impossible for me to go home with father. I knew that the man would manage to persuade my father, that father was too soft-hearted, that he would give in. I prepared myself for whatever would happen and fell asleep.

The next day I felt so happy, knowing that I would see my father again. My chores were nothing to me, and I did them in no time. The hours went by, and the couple came home. They, too, felt my happiness; I guess I was glowing all over. I couldn't help but notice that I had not felt so elated in a long time. I still knew how to be happy.

Father, Please Take Me Home

Father arrived at the same time as the day before. He visited for a couple of hours and, as I expected, was persuaded to allow me to stay on. The man offered to take him back to the ship and said that I could come along. When we reached the ship, the man held on to the side to keep the canoe anchored. Father didn't move out of the canoe, but faced me and spoke, "Be kind, be patient, and take care of your responsibilities well. If you are confronted with unpleasantness, do not respond the same way. If you will be good to people, they will be good to you, and most of all, do not be *makkutuk*," a soft-headed teenager.

While father was advising me, my only answers were yes, yes, and yes. I could see the man was beginning to tire of holding on to the ship. Father's last words were, "Just be patient, you will come home again soon." My heart was heavy, tears bursting out of my eyes, and my mind crying, "Father, please take me home!" We arrived back at the dock and I helped the man pull the canoe to the land. I started walking back to the house, and the man caught up with me. I was so glad that it was dark, I did not want him to see my tears. No doubt he was relieved that father let me stay on. I made no comments whatever, and we reached the house. His wife was in bed with her door open. "Pretty happy day, eh, Minnie?" she said as I passed. I stopped for a second and gave her a smile, then went into my bedroom. I was tired from crying silently in the canoe, from the anxiety I had endured, hoping father would have the strength to insist that I go home.

Father had His Own Reason

The next day passed as if there had been no excitement during the previous couple of days. I forced myself to do my chores. The two children kept my energy running and my day interesting. They helped me to forget my father and my home. But I would sit and think, trying to figure out what my father had planned to do before he came to see me. No doubt he had come to see what kind of life I was leading or growing into. Probably he had planned to take me home for good, so that his worries about my marriage would end. To him, and according to our customs, I should have been married and having my own children to strengthen our Inuit group, to contribute to our economy. All that is very important to Inuit fathers. Yet his loving heart and his capacity to see that his daughter was needed by others made him give up the thought of taking me home. And, as long as there was peace, he was going to be peaceful too.

Years later, I found out why he did not fight to take me home. After grandfather Weetaltuk's death, the James Bay group had no leader, no one who kept them together. They had tried to elect Weetaltuk's oldest son as the leader, but he was not strong like his father and had been ailing. Both his youngest son and my father were too young, and neither was outspoken enough to be able to lead other adults. They would have been taken advantage of all the time had they tried. At this time, too, the qallunaat from the Department of Northern Affairs were asking the James Bay group to move to Great Whale River. Father felt at the time that nothing was right at home, there was no solid base. Everything was in upheaval. There was no security left among them, and father did not want me to come home to that. As father put it, "Our home was nalunartuq," hard to understand, future unknown, solid security missing. It was as though my group had dispersed into nothing, the proud people were no more. Grandfather had taken it all with him when he died. So, father did have reasons for not taking me home.

My father has never expressed regret or happiness about my marriage into another culture. As always, he gave me only advice. "Do what pleases him, and he will please you, too. Don't arouse him to something you will regret. You may not always know it, but you will be the foundation of your home, it will be up to you how that foundation stands. You are the woman, the mother, who is capable of making the marriage successful. If you show goodness to him, he will return it to you."

Somehow I do not believe that advice; it does not work in the qallunaat culture. Father did not know that qallunaat men are not like Inuit men. I have tested his advice to see if it works. I have learned that some *qallunaat* men do not know how to appreciate goodness in their wives, do not know how to return goodness to them. I have learned that the nicer you are and the more willing to cater to them without complaint, the more they think they have a regular maid or even a slave. I am not saying that every *qallunaat* marriage is that way. I, too, have learned to argue, to fight, and to tell my *qallunaaq* husband loud and clear that while I am his maid in many ways I, too, like to be served. To me, slavery has an entirely different meaning than working hard physically every-day. I would feel like a slave if my affections were not returned, when what I have done to improve my household and motherly duties were not noticed, when whatever I made was not com-plimented by my husband. To me, marriage is a very private venture among the many adventures of life.

Harmony is not Forever

After my father's visit, the summer came into full bloom. I felt happier now that I had seen him. I performed my responsibilities well, and I could tell that the couple appreciated my services. The children were my reward, my company, and they made me feel that I was a worthwhile person. But fixed happiness and rewards are not meant to stay forever. There is always something trying to interfere or ruin a state of harmony.

One afternoon there was a knock at the front door, and I went to answer it. Who should be at the door but the instigator. I was glad to see her and was excited by this surprise visit. I had not seen her for almost five years. Over tea we sat and discussed many things, the many people that we knew and our relatives. She asked me about my job, my pay, about the couple, and what I planned to do later. It seemed she had changed and had grown up. After I had told her everything, her manner became impish, and that old mischievous shine was in her eyes. Though I did not show it, I felt apprehensive inside me while she went on, "Min-nie, you don't have to be here, these people don't own you, you don't have to be a maid, you don't have to earn measly pay. You are Weetaltuk's granddaughter, you can do better than this. Why don't you come with me back to Hamilton and finish nursing? Why don't you get another job with better pay? You don't have to look after someone else's brats, you don't have to do without nice clothes, and you don't have to stay here at Moose!"

I knew she was right in many ways, but I couldn't help but think that she had not really changed. She was still her old self, she thought of no one but herself, she did things for her own gain. All she had on her mind was me, me, me, and mine, mine, mine. She became quiet, because I was not responding. Suddenly she remembered that she had a date with one of the pilots who had flown in that morning. She was proud to tell me that, because she knew I was not as open and forward as she was. She knew that I had been there almost two years, and still I had no steady boy-friend.

She left as unexpectedly as she came. Though I was glad to see her, as she was one of my Inuit group, I soon forgot her again. She did not forget me, though. Probably she wondered about me long after she left. A few days later, a letter was found by the woman, written to her husband, saying that I was madly in love with him, and supposedly signed by me. I could not begin to describe all that it said. I tried to deny the whole thing to both of them, but she took it very seriously. He only laughed. The more suspicious she became, the more he teased me in front of her.

He knew that he was not guilty, but did his wife know? I could not believe that she did not know her own husband after all those years. I could not understand why she did not believe me. "But you signed the letter," she kept reminding me. But I did not write it, was all I could say. And he just made it worse. I could see that the more suspicious she was, the more he got a kick out of the whole thing. It was as though he was enjoying her jealousy.

The dismal fall weather seemed to arrive so quickly. The grey skies, rain, and sleet made me feel dismal, too. I went out more often to visit friends, to get away from the suspicions of the woman. She was tearing apart my relationship to every one of them, including the children. Though she did not bring up the subject, I could see that she did not trust me. She watched every move I made. I was dying inside; she was killing my natural innocent behaviour. Sometimes at nights, after we had gone to bed, I would hear her questioning her husband. He would be so gentle and give her all the expressions of love that he had for her. I would fall asleep while she still questioned him.

Though their waking, eating, and work habits were the same, her suspicions lingered on. She did not have to speak them, but I felt them anyway. I did not have that happy willingness to serve her anymore. I did not want to greet her husband when he came home, afraid that she might read something into it. I had no more desire to be there, I had no wish to live amidst ugly feelings. I decided that I would talk to both of them about leaving when they had calmed down. I knew the happy relations that I had built so patiently and quietly were no more. I learned that jealousy and suspicion created for no reason are very destructive to human relations. Harmony is not forever.

Did the Drink Drive Me Crazy?

Winter was soon half over, and Christmas was in the air. I ordered a set of dishes from Eaton's to give to the couple. Though I had always known Christmas to be a happy occasion, I felt heavy in heart. Between the woman and I existed an artificial relationship. I kept waiting for the right moment to tell them that I wanted to leave, but I had a lot of things to think about first, before I could tell them. I had no place to go. I had no other job. I did not want to move in with any of my friends. I could not go home as there were no planes or ships running. I felt utterly stuck. I had to think a bit more. I put the whole thing at the back of my mind and tried to run the household as best I could. At least the children helped cheer me up, and they brightened my grey days.

It was two days before Christmas Eve. Everybody seemed to be in a happy state of mind; I, most of all, tried to keep them that way. The couple gave me a day off before Christmas so that I could babysit when they went out Christmas Eve. I did not mind that. I was used to it and expected nothing else. I had no special friends with whom to celebrate the occasion.

The couple went out as planned; the children and I were alone. We were sitting in the living room, playing games. They became silly, and instead of trying to control their silliness, I joined them. I had not had a release of fun like this for a long time, and I was enjoying the whole thing. Though their bed time was overdue, I did not put them to bed. The little boy, who was always sillier, ran over to a small bookcase. On the top of the bookcase was a carafe of liquor. It was always there, always full, and the husband and wife dipped into it every now and then. But they had never offered me any, nor was I anxious that they should. I was never tempted to try it; as far as I was concerned, it belonged to the man and his wife.

The boy began to pour the liquor into one of the glasses that sat by the carafe. I ran over to him and told him not to touch it. As I was taking it out of his little hands, the smell of the liquor hit my nose. The little boy was urging, "Here, Minnie, drink it." I took a small sip, as I was a little scared of it. Somewhere I had heard that this kind of drink made you crazy. I took another sip, and each time my throat would burn and sting. Will I really go crazy? Maybe not. I had not seen the couple go crazy. I took another sip, but still I did not feel crazy. The little boy had filled the glass. I drank until it was empty. My body began to feel warm; I felt light, and became sillier with the children. The liquor was beginning to work on me.

I forgot all about the time, and the children did not know any better. As far as they were concerned they were loose. Suddenly the front door opened, and the couple walked in. I hugged them both and wished them a merry Christmas. The wife started screaming, giving me hell and telling me that I was fired. I could hear her husband trying to calm her down, telling her to put the children to bed. She kept accusing me of harming the children. Then he would speak, "Make some coffee and get it into her. She doesn't know or understand a thing you are saying. Can't you see her condition? Calm down, will you?" She went to make coffee, but I refused it. The man spoke to me slowly, as though he were trying to reach the sensible part of my mind. "Minnie, you don't want the children to see you like this, do you?" He knew what to say, knew what I cared about. "You know where your bedroom is? Go to bed. My wife and I will speak to you tomorrow." I got up and went to bed, clothes and all.

I must have been in a stupor, as I could not remember anything until the next morning. I woke slowly and moved around a bit on my bed. My body was stiff and my head was thumping and aching. I felt sick in my stomach. I lay down again. I wondered what the couple would do to me. They will be so mad, they will give me hell, fire me, maybe. I was so ashamed and began to hope that they would fire me.

Finally I got up and the couple began to talk to me. "Minnie, we don't like what you did here last night, we are hoping that you won't do it again. On that basis we have decided to keep you." Since they were being so understanding, I wanted to apologize, I wanted to tell them that I had not planned it that way, that I just meant to have fun with the children. I wanted to tell them that I became curious about the drink, to see if it would drive me crazy, but I could not. They reminded me that I could have easily harmed the children. That was the end of that. It was forgotten, though I was very disappointed that they did not let me go.

Grandmother was Always Right

The new year of 1956 arrived, and my home kept coming to my mind. I decided that I would tell the couple to start looking for someone long before I left; that way, they would have no reason to hold me back. I kept waiting for the right moment. One night the woman and I were alone in the house, and the children were asleep. Her husband had gone to Moosonee to arrange some orders for the confectionery. I thought it was going to be one of those evenings when we might sit and chat about anything, but it was not so. She asked me bluntly if I loved her husband. What could I say? I had been taught to love many ways. I did not know how to answer her silly question. I did not want to say no, because I did love the man in the way I would love anyone who had been a good guardian to me. And I did not want to say yes, either, because she would not understand what kind of love I meant.

Of course, she did not wait for an answer but went on. "You could make him happier since you understand his native ways. His parents would probably accept you better." I could not believe my ears. She was still thinking about that crazy letter, written by someone who was as crazy as her. Finally I spoke "Tomorrow I am going to look for another job." That was all I said, and then I went to bed. She tried to speak to me, but I wouldn't hear her. Tears were running down my cheeks which made it harder for me to face her. Her last words were, "Minnie, you can't do this to me. I'm sure you will feel better tomorrow." My mind was determined that I would not give in, no matter what she or he said to me. I would turn my soft heart to stone and think of me, me, me and mine, mine, mine.

The next morning I made my way to the school, rehearsing in my mind what I was going to say to whoever I met there. Near the door was a sign that read "Principal." There, inside the office, sat a very thin man behind a desk. We startled each other, but he greeted me politely. "What can I do for you?" he asked. "I am looking for a job," I replied. "What would you like to do?" I didn't know, but I was willing to do anything. "Who is your present employer?" I told him. "Why are you leaving?" I was not happy there. He sat back in his chair. "I don't know if I have anything that you could handle on your own. We do have two openings, one in the laundry. The matron is going to have a baby and plans not to return to work. The other is supervising forty-four intermediate girls. I don't think you can handle forty-four children – some of them are bigger than you. No, you don't look tough enough. Would you like to try the laundry?" I said yes; in fact, I just about sang it out. "Fine," he said. "Do you have a place to stay?" No. "Then you can move to the staff rooms, that will be even better for everyone. Come on Monday, first thing in the morning. I will speak to the matron who will show you what has to be done." I felt too shy to thank him, so I just gave him an appreciative smile. I was leaving his office when he spoke, "You can move in during the weekend or even today, if you like," I was so relieved.

I decided to move right away, the sooner the better. I said nothing and went straight to my room to pack. There was a knock at my door, and the woman hurried in. She wanted to know if I had had anything to eat, and I said no. She wanted me to come to the kitchen and said that she would fix me something. She tried to give me a smile which I did not want to return. Then she began, "Minnie, I can't do without you. Look at the house, look at my kitchen sink, the children will miss you." I did not answer. I was afraid that I would begin to feel sorry for her again and probably stay on till next summer. That summer was so long away. She kept on, "Minnie, we have made up in the past, let's make up now and forget everything." I did not answer and kept on packing. Finally she closed the door, and I could hear her talking to her husband, trying to urge him to talk to me, but he never came to my door. He knew he had had enough nonsense, too. I was glad that he had a native nature and that he understood how people felt, how much people can take, that people can be pushed only so far.

I finished packing. I wanted to hug the children and tell them where I was going. But I could not. I headed straight for the front door and closed it behind me. I felt neither happy nor remorseful. I had never thought that I would leave that way. I had always imagined that when the time came for me to leave these people, who had taken me in, who had come to care about my well-being, would see me off to the ship as friends forever. But, like grand-mother always said, some things don't stay the same forever, and one can't plan to stay the same forever. Grandmother was always right when it came to human nature.

Machines are Cold

I moved into the school just as lunch was being served. I had not eaten the whole morning, but I was not hungry. I was shown to my room and introduced to the rest of the staff. Though the principal did not live at the school, he, too, came to the dining room to welcome me. I felt very shy, as usual, and could not express myself. I just smiled and thought to myself that here was another life for me to get used to.

The children were many. Though I didn't have anything to do with them, I still had to handle their clothes. There were six senior boys, twenty-six juniors, twenty-four senior girls, forty-four intermediates, and forty-two juniors. There were six supervisors, two workers in the kitchen, one nurse, one engineer and his wife who managed choir singing, one janitor, whose wife was pregnant and had to give up the laundry, one sewing room matron, and four teachers. Neither the minister and his wife, nor the principal and his wife lived in the school. There were two outside helpers who came in everyday, one for the sewing room and one for the laundry.

I prepared my mind to my new job. I planned to do it well. My father's voice came to me, as it always did when I was confronted with a new situation. "Work with patience, and learn all you can." Though I had not worked in a big laundry, I knew a lot about washing clothes by now. I knew about different fabrics and had learned which kinds shrink and which ones run their colours. My day started at nine o'clock every morning and ended at five in the afternoon. My pay was seventy-five dollars a month. I spent the weekend just settling in. I organized my room, and prepared my daily clothing. I wanted my room to be in order, so that I would always feel relaxed there. I could see that I was going to be in it a lot, since I was too shy to mingle with the other staff so soon. Though I love people and would rather be among people I know well, I have always been very slow to open up to them.

Monday morning arrived. I was up at seven. I glanced out the window; the weather still looked cold. I washed and dressed. As I was a live-in employee I had to conform to the school rules. After breakfast everyone went to the chapel for prayer service. From there the staff went to their jobs and the children went over to the classrooms, which were right next door. When I found my way to the laundry room the former matron was already there. She was pleasant and showed me around the laundry. There were three big steel washing machines, two dryers, one bed sheet presser, two sinks, and lots of little boards and hand irons. The matron explained the procedure and told me what was expected. "You will like it here. It's noisy, but you will enjoy it," she said. She wished me luck and left.

I began to divide the different colours. I looked inside the big machines and made an eye judgement to see how much I should put in each machine. I had wondered earlier how I could finish all this laundry in eight hours. Now I could see that it was possible. The machines just seemed to devour the clothing. Around 10:00 A.M. the sewing room matron came in and asked if I would like to have a break for coffee. I was not a coffee drinker at the time, but I did not refuse her as she was an elderly woman. She, too, like the nurse, had a motherly look and was practically bald. She introduced herself as we were walking towards the dining room; her name was the same as the principal's. He was her son. He had come to Canada from England, and she followed four years later. "Yes, I left my old home, all my friends, so I am a stranger here," she said. "At least you are at home," she commented. I told her that I was not really home either. I tried to tell her where my home was, but she had no idea.

By noon I had the whole laundry done, all that remained was the drying, ironing and folding. The afternoon went very fast. As the day drew to a close, I thought about the couple's home and especially about the wife. I felt glad to have left. I opened the laundry room door and looked back in to make sure everything was in order. The machines were cold, but at least they would not hurt my feelings, ever!

They were Strangers more than I

Although I was happy at the laundry and willing to do my job well, my mind yearned for more challenge. I was beginning to find that I could turn my mind on and off just like the machines. My reflexes became automatic, and I knew in my heart that it was not for me. I knew that I needed something new to get rid of my energies.

One day, as I was taking my break with the other staff, my ears perked up when I heard one of the supervisors complaining about her job. Apparently the children were giving her a lot of trouble. She was about to see the principal and had decided to quit her job. It gave me an idea. That same evening I went down to her bed-room, which was between two dorms of intermediate girls. I had come to know her, so she asked me to come in.

Her room was a dreadful mess! There were piles of clothes in almost every corner of her room — stockings, aprons, underwear and tunics. No wonder she was not happy. Grandmother had always said, if you want to be happy within yourself, keep your living area in order. She apologized for the mess and I made no comment. I sat down and asked if she would consider switching jobs. She almost jumped to the idea. Then she asked me if my job was hard and I said no; it was noisy, but not hard. She thought a little more, then spoke again, "Do you think you can handle the disobedience of forty-four brats?" I said that I was willing to change if she was. We made an agreement that we could always change back if it did not work out. We decided to go and see the principal the next morning during our coffee breaks.

Together we went to the principal's office and came right out with what we wanted. The principal talked to us individually. To me he said, "Minnie, you are so small, smaller than some of those intermediate girls. They are hard to handle, you are so young and look too gentle. They will run all over you! Besides, I have not heard one complaint from the staff about shrunken sweaters since you came to the laundry." It looked like he would not go for the idea. I felt very disappointed and did not try to hide it. He became silent. Finally he said that he had to keep his staff happy and agreed that I could try. If the children were too much for me, I could always change back to the laundry. The principal wished us both lots of luck.

During Sunday supper the principal introduced me to all the children. The principal asked for attention and spoke, "You children all know Miss Aodla. She has been your laundry matron, but now she is going to supervise the intermediate girls. You intermediates will have to listen to her, obey her orders and rules, tell her when you have problems, tell her when you feel sick. As you can see, she is small. If you give her any troubles, she will come to me." I could see that he was still very doubtful, and he put doubts on the faces of these children. But I was determined.

I went up to the second floor, to my new room, which was now half empty, though all the children's clothing was still scattered about. There was a knock at my door; it was the former supervisor. She wanted to know if I would take the children to the Sunday church service that evening in the village. I said yes and she left with a look of relief. I had to think fast. I had one hour to ready myself, but it was not just me that I had to think about — I had forty-four others to consider. My girls were all downstairs in the playroom. I made myself neat and went down. I opened the playroom door, and the noise of many languages came to my ears. Some were speaking their own Indian language and some, English. They noticed me, and there was silence. I told the intermediates to line up, to go up to their dorm room, and to change into their Sunday service clothing. They all obeyed right away. I wondered if it would always be as easy as this, but I knew it was only temporary obedience. On the stairs the line broke up, and they all started to chatter. They knew this was not the rule; already they were testing me. I did not say anything. I wanted to wait for a better time to remind them about the school rules.

I went to my own room, more or less to see if they knew how to prepare themselves for church. It was not so; some of them came to my door, wanting to know what to wear, to show me their torn stockings or unstitched dresses. I knew that the principal insisted on the children being on time. I told them to wear what they had, and that I would see to them in the coming week. I got into my own coat and lined them up in the dorm hall. My heart sank as I began to notice their coats; some were torn, some had buttons missing, and some did not fit anymore. But we had to get moving. As we walked towards the church, I felt ashamed to see these children in their tattered clothes. I knew that for many years the residential schools were always talked about by the villagers — how the school children ate poorly, wore rags, and that the school did not really look after them well. I decided right there that I would not be a part of it. By next Sunday the children's clothes would be in better condition.

Before bedtime that night I had a few moments to speak to them. I reminded them that there was silence on the stairs, that if chatter happened again I would punish not just the culprit, but all of them. At this point, I did not know what I was going to use for punishment, but I took a chance. As we went up, not one strayed out of line, and no one dared speak. From then on I knew that if I were willing to make my rules stick, the children would eventually conform to them without hate. They washed and brushed their teeth, and all went to their beds. I said goodnight, and the chorus came back, "Good night, Miss Aodla," and I turned off the lights.

As soon as I had disappeared into my room, whispers began in the darkness of the dorms. I stood for a while and thought. Should I ignore it or do something about it? I decided to do something. I went to one of the dorms and switched on the light. All was silence. I could see that they were sneaky. I asked who was whispering, but no one dared to answer. I was not satisfied, so I said, "Okay, you will all have to supervise yourselves tomorrow while I sleep all day!" All heads were raised and eyes turned to one girl. I went to her. I asked for her name and made her stand in the centre of the floor. "See all these girls? You are keeping them awake. They want to sleep so they can have a good rest." I knew that she had no sense of responsibility for the needs of the others, but I also knew that she did not like to stand out in front of all those eyes. I told her to return to her bed and to go to sleep. I heard no more whispers.

The next morning I got up and dressed. When I went into the

dorms, some of the girls were already awake, enjoying their beds without a sound. I could see which of them were going to cause problems in the mornings in terms of speed. I went back and forth between the two dorms, encouraging them to hurry a little. I assembled them for the dining room, and then I went to have my own breakfast. Every staff member had something to say as I entered. "How is it going, Minnie? How are you going to manage all those girls?" I made no comment, just smiled and ate. But I was determined to get rid of their doubts, to demonstrate that my smallness had nothing to do with my capabilities.

That very day, when classes and supper were over, I asked the girls to come up to their dorms. I had every one of them take their beds apart and told them to turn over their mattresses and clean their bedside tables. I told them to put everything that they did not need or personally own in the centre of the floor. Everything went flying as the mattresses were turned over — paper, old rags, soiled underwear, socks without mates, crayons and chalk. We did not stop until everything was spic and span. I tried to make the whole clean-up a happy event, and they soon caught on.

As the time went by, I won the girls' cooperation. I never stood around to order them. Whenever there was something to be done, I involved myself with them. I got to know each of their individual ways, some tried to be smart, some were even-tempered, some tried to tattletale, and some tried to avoid their work. I ignored nothing and always got to the bottom of whatever they tried. I never screamed or scolded. When I had to punish them, I did it right in front of all the others. They hated that and felt shy and ashamed. I never made any promises to them that I could not keep. I used all the methods of obedience that I had learned from my grandmother, and I fell in love with all of them. I hugged them when I felt it was the right moment. I gave them compliments to encourage their efforts.

When I got together with the other staff, all wondered how I could manage those girls without difficulties. All said that it was the first time they had seen the intermediates looking neat, always on time, and behaving during chapel service. I just thanked them. They didn't realize that I had some advantages over them. I spoke four languages, two of which all the children understood. I also knew some of the girls' parents, some of their sisters and brothers had gone to this same school with me. I said nothing, and I had no time to explain long stories. They had no time to listen either. They never realized that they were strangers more than I. Some were from England, from Scotland, from Toronto, from Woodstock, Ontario, and even one from the United States.

The Agent was Still After Me

Spring was in the air again, but I was not thinking about home as I was too busy. The children were talking about their homes, though; they would be so glad when school was over. It sounded familiar to hear them talk about their homes, just as I used to think about home when I was their age. I could not help but share their emotions in my private thoughts. I began to plan. Yes, I would go home that summer when all the children had left. Yes, I would tell the principal at the end of the school year. I felt elated. I knew that the principal had no reason to hold me there. He had all summer to replace me.

It was almost the end of April, 1957. I began to take the girls for long walks when we had nothing else to do. Sometimes, on my days off, I went down to the river. It was on one of those walks to the river that I ran into the Indian agent. He stopped me. He wanted me to come with him to his office. He was serious, more stern than usual, and he did not melt with the humour I attempted. We reached his office, and he told me to sit on a chair. He wasted no time and began, "The people in Ottawa still want you. They need a translator right away. If I were you, I would go. Not many girls in your situation get an opportunity like this. I am telling you, you should go. I will lend you the money for the fare and accommodation. I'll make all the arrangements. I'll even go and see the principal myself and tell him about it. Okay?" I began to object, but he would not hear me and told me to go, that he would let me know when everything was arranged.

I walked back to the school thinking. Surely I will get home before he has a chance to make any arrangements. Some of these *qallunaat* talk a lot without ever doing what they say they are going to do. Or so I thought! In a couple of days, the principal called me down to his office. He said that he had been very happy with my services, that not many could take my place, but. . . . He used the very words of the agent, and that was that. I had one week to get ready; other supervisors would take turns to tend the intermediates until the end of the school year. As for me, I had to pack, think and plan all over again.

It was now the second of May, and the ice on the river was long gone. The two elderly women, the nurse and the sewing room matron, came with two other supervisors to take me to the other side to Moosonee where I would catch my train. I was very glad that we did not have to stand and wait around as my throat was in pain, needing to cry. I boarded, and my friends were no more. It was a long ride to North Bay where I had to stay overnight. The hotel knew who I was, and a bellboy showed me my room. I was glad that he left quickly. I wanted to be alone to think. What was I doing? I felt tired and went straight to bed.

The phone wakened me. Yes? "It is 7:00 o'clock," the voice said. I dressed and looked out the window. All I could see was cement and many parked cars. The weather looked warm and the sky so blue. Soon I was on my way again, heading for Ottawa. I sat and looked out the window. I saw many strange things and wondered if all these things would eventually push into my Inuit land. I shivered as I saw a polluted river, tall buildings, and many, many cars.

Everything was cement and metal. Hours went by until I arrived at Ottawa. It was scary, noisy, smelly and so very strange. I knew that I was strange, too, because everybody was staring at me while I stood waiting for the man who was supposed to pick me up. This was how I arrived in southern Canada, learning all over again about fear, sadness, gladness, disappointment, excitement, lovingness, and rewards; to wonder, to gain, to care, to humour, to lose and meet many people, to have an adventure among these *qallunaat*.

How Do I Like the Weather?

Twenty-one years have passed since that trying day. I am used to many things by now. I am immune to the weather by now. I have found ways to cool myself during heat waves. Sometimes I'm even cold during winter. *Upinnarani!* It is no wonder! I am dressed like a *qallunaat* lady, just a coat, no head wear, and flimsy little stockings. I have learned that I am not dependent on the weather, like I used to be when I was a nomad. I don't have to take my furnishings along every time I want to travel. For that, the weather is just fine. I have decided, though, that there is no spring in the South. Spring, to me, is when the snow begins to melt slowly, when I can see and hear streams running into one another, when the mass of ice begins to show huge cracks, when I hear geese flying over my head, when I begin to run outside without a heavy parka, when I see hunters dressed in white, stalking basking seals in the sun, when I see wild, tiny flowers blooming. That is the kind of weather I miss, and I miss my dear people who are becoming stranger, even to me, covering their familiar ways with another culture.

About the author

Minnie Aodla Freeman was born in 1936 on Cape Hope Island in James Bay. At the age of sixteen, she commenced nurse's training at Ste. Therese School in Fort George, and in 1957 she went to Ottawa to accept a position as a translator with the then Department of Northern Affairs and National Resources.

Today a writer and translator, Mrs. Freeman has published poems and short stories in the *Canadian Children's Annual,* and a number of commissioned works were included in the International Women's Year travelling exhibition. A play , "Survival in the South," was produced for the Dominion Drama Festival in 1971 and was staged at the National Arts Centre, Ottawa, in 1973. *Life Among the Qallunaat* is her first book.

Design/David Shaw & Associates Ltd.
Jacket illustration/Vlasta van Kampen
Typesetting/Modern Composition Ltd.
Printing & Binding/John Deyell Company